This publication is designed to provide accurate authoritative information in regard to the subject matter covered. It is sold with the understanding that the publisher is not engaged in rendering legal, accounting, or other professional services. If legal advice or other expert assistance is required the services of a competent professional should be sought.

Some of the methods presented in this book may be illegal in certain parts of the United States. This book is sold for information purposes only.

ISBN 0-933301-50-2

FINANCIAL SUCCESS

MONEY
Making Reports

7th Edition

Including
$200,000 In
24 Hours

Table of Contents

Introduction 7

1) Marketing Your Company 9
— Advertising And Promoting Your Business
— Money From Your Importing Business
— Loans And Grants For Your Business

**2) How To Run A Business And Collect Income
At Home** 65
— Cash Through The Mail
— Cash From Your Telephone
— Cash From Magazine And Newspaper
Advertisements
— Savings And Investments
— Establishing And Using Credit To Your Advantage
— Unique Businesses

**3) How To Make And Save Money On Your
Home And Automobiles** 115

4) Information You Can Collect Free 131
— Free Goods And Services
— Great Ideas And Secrets

INTRODUCTION

Have you ever thought: "There must be an easier way?" If this feeling is all too familiar to you, you'll be interested in the 130 ways to ease your financial burdens, to start up interesting and inexpensive businesses, and to increase your overall knowledge of just what is out there for you, and how to go about getting it.

Many people get stuck in a cycle of bad debts, bad credit, poor planning and lack of foresight in starting up a business, and consequently develop a poor self-image of themselves. They continue to be unaware that there are ways out of this trap. The problem is, many people become so desperate that they not only lose the ability to think innovatively, but they begin to expect magical cures for all of their debt problems. This book provides no magical cures, but instead, offers many previously unrecognized start-up ideas for various kinds of business ventures. It is full of up-to-date references with the names and addresses of people just like you, who have pulled themselves out of debt, put in some hard work and time, and are now involved in successful businesses which they, themselves, own and operate.

If you have asked yourself too many times—"Why can't I get ahead?"—it is time that you start reading and applying these innovative methods to your own life. Remember: The road to financial security and financial self-fulfillment starts with positive thinking, planning and action. Let's begin.

Section One

Advertising And Promoting Your Company

Marketing Your Company

Trying to save too much money can have a bad effect on your business. When you are trying to save money, do not give your company a cheap appearance. Don't try to cut corners with your sales literature, or by having cheap looking stationery or direct mail pieces. Your prospect's first impression of your company is determined by the mailing piece you send him. He will assume that the product you send him will be the same quality as the mailing piece he got. Companies spend a great deal of money for *four-color jobs* so they can impress you. If they can afford good mailing pieces, are you going to doubt their products? If you give people the impression that they are dealing with a high-class company, you will increase your profits. It is not wise to overdo your company, to give it a high-class image.

Type Everything

All of your sales letters, press releases, name labels, etc., should be typed. Handwriting should be used as little as possible. If you do not have a typewriter, rent or buy one.

Create A Distinct Company Image

All big companies have a distinct company image, a logo. Create a logo for your company. A logo will give you that high-class image of a large company. It also helps your customers find your ads. We are sure that many of you may want to create a logo for your company. Make sure your logos look neat and professional. To have your logo created, look up graphic designers in the Yellow Pages. If you have a hard time finding a suitable artist, take advantage of my logo creating service. One of my talented artists will create your artistic, personalized, camera-ready logo for only $60. The logo will be shipped to you as soon as possible; if you are not satisfied with it, send it back and another will be designed at no extra charge. Send $60 to Success Graphics, 6150 Mission Gorge Road, Ste. 231, San Diego, Calif, 92120.

Give Your Company A Distinct Name

People will relate your company name to your products and services. What you name your company can affect sales. If your name is Steve Smith and you sell books, what should you call your company? You will get more orders if you call your company Smith Publishers than if you called your company Steve Smith. If you sell paper, you might call yourself Smith Paper Co.

Typeset Your Sales Material

If you are planning to circulate a mailing piece or you are placing an ad in a publication, do not type it on a typewriter, typeset it. An exception to this rule is a sales letter. Get a professional to prepare your ad, since it will be worth it in the long run.

Getting Rich In Mail-Order

There is an excellent series of books on the market which can teach you everything you need to know to make money in the mail order business. The series is called *Direct Response Millions* and is available from Lion Publishing Co., at 6150 Mission Gorge Rd., #225, San Diego, Calif, 92120.

This series begins with information on starting a mail order company, from explaining the benefits of the system, such as reaching your desired market and personalized service, to discussing how to select a printing press for your materials. Different methods of fulfillment are also reviewed. You may want to stock your own warehouse and fill orders yourself, or you might consider using the services of a "fulfillment company" to receive your goods and ship to your customers, bypassing you completely and freeing you to discover new mail markets.

Advertising is the most important aspect of a mail order business, and these books cover many types of advertising. You will learn to write display and classified ads that really pull in business. Also discussed are how to get free advertising via press releases and magazine articles. Any information which is presented in a "newsy" or very straightforward manner can win you free publicity by attracting different media.

If you choose to offer a product rather than a service, you will find many different ideas in this series about where to find inexpensive suppliers of many different and unique items, both foreign and abroad. If you are interested in designing and patenting your own product, this series will show you how to go about researching past ideas, which you may be able to cash in on, or how to create your own products. It also designates the correct paths to take to patent or copyright a product and to get a trademark for your new company.

You will learn, too, how the government helps small businesses, such as new mail order suppliers, with consultant advice, tax breaks, and even low interest loans supplied by the federal government. The complicated process of dealing with the government is also simplified.

I highly recommend this series. Its wealth of information is based on competent research and years of field experience. You will find it to be more valuable than any other book on your shelf.

"Use Your Hidden Potential To Get Rich"

I recommend that everyone who wants to make money should have a copy of this book, quoted as being the best on making money. It presents a program that clearly maps the route self-made millionaires took to make their fortunes. Every millionaire has used the techniques in this book to achieve success.

Hidden Potential will show any individual, regardless of skill, intelligence and experience, how to use their mind to realize both their business and their personal dreams.

This book is illustrated with charts and diagrams that guide you through the wealth-mind transformation process. Included are quizzes which monitor your progress to wealth. The author, David Bendah, backs up his points with interesting examples of how ordinary people—from Milton Hershey to William Colgate—used the same techniques to make fortunes. Bendah also devotes three chapters to Japanese wealth-building techniques. In short, this volume is designed to expose the reader to every success principle needed to get rich. The results of his book have been proven beyond a doubt. If you are serious about making money, this book is a must. This book is available for only $12.00 plus $1 (postage and handling) from Lion Publishing Company, 6150 Mission Gorge Road, Suite 225, San Diego, Calif, 92120.

Where You Should Advertise

One of the best ways to sell reports is through the classifieds. Go to your local newsstand and check through magazines that carry classified advertising space. Magazines such as "Popular Science", "Field and Stream", "Outdoor Life", "The National Enquirer", etc., or any magazine where you find a great deal of advertising, is a good bet for you. After you locate the magazine of your choice, find out what the rates are. The rates are sometimes listed right in the magazine. Write to the magazine if you can't locate the rates. Ask for its Mail- Order Classified & Display Rate Cards. The address should be in the inside cover. These cards should give you all the information you need to place an ad. You may also decide that you want to sell these reports through a mailing list. We know of one good company that can sell you high quality, fresh "Opportunity Seeker" names at a good price. All of its names come on pressure sensitive labels. Prices are as follows: 250 names for $35. To get them, write to Lion Publishing Co. 6150 Mission Gorge Rd, Ste. 225, San Diego, Calif 92120.

If you would like more information about how to advertise in classified or display advertisements, you may want to consider a book called "Making Money From Display & Classified Ads" which is produced by Lion Publishing Co. You can get a copy by sending them $15.00 at 6150 Mission Gorge Rd., #225, San Diego, Calif, 92120

How To Make Money Even When Your Ads Don't Pull

Step one: Advertise in a mail-order magazine that you can co-publish. The price will be the same as the ad the first time alone—usually a 50% discount thereafter.

Step two: With the copies you receive as co-publisher you can make money because you receive 50% commission on ads, subscriptions, etc., that are placed through you. We co-publish magazines which we make a profit on, even when our ads don't pull, and you can, too. It's a great way to test new ads and eliminate those that don't pull.

Step three: Distribute your magazine to people who are likely to place ads, etc. Check for firms who advertise in one co-publisher magazine and not in another. Send them a copy of your magazine they are not currently co-publishing or advertising. Since the publisher's name is not printed on the magazine, readers will have to order through you. When they do, you make 50% and more.

How To Get Your 3 x 6 Circulars Typeset Free

The plan is so simple you'll wonder why you never thought of it yourself. But once you give it a try, you will thank us a thousand times for revealing it to you. There are literally hundreds of mail-order publications that will print your ad by the "letterpress" method. This means they actually set it up in type. This is the only method that an ad or a circular can be done properly and with good taste (commercial art excepted, of course). First, pick out a good publication and determine the words per inch. If your offer has any merit at all, your ad in either MAIL SALE ADVERTISER or MAIL-ORDER DISCOUNTER, will sell for you many times over the price of the ad. This means your ad is run for free. And, after your ad is published in the magazine, you merely clip it out, mail it to your printer, and presto—you have your ad or 3 x 6 circular typeset for FREE—plus you've made a good profit.

How To Turn Old Newspapers Into Cash Dollars

Scan your newspaper every day for headlines and advertisement layouts that contain catchy or interesting phrases in bold, well-printed type. You may use printing that is either black and white, or red and white. The next step is to use these headlines on circulars. Finish the body of your circular with your typewriter. You can make some really fine "camera ready" copy by doing this. Clip cartoons and "cute" drawings and incorporate them into your ads. Practice this and you will soon have the expertise to compose ads and paste-ups for other dealers. Sell this service and you can make good money. This plan can soon grow into a well-paying career.

How To Write A Great Ad

The Headline

The most important part of an ad is the headline. Research tells us that 80% of the success of an ad depends on the headline. The headline should catch the attention of your readers. Once you get their attention, your "copy" sells them your product or service. There are many ways to write a headline. The most effective headlines are filled with reader benefits. It is important to understand that people are selfish. If there is nothing in it for them, they will not respond to your ad. The headline is going to tell your prospects what you are going to do for them. It has to portray a definite benefit. 'It's Fun to Make Money the Easy Way' is a headline lacking the essential benefit to the reader. A person reading this headline will look at it, agree with it, and then move on to another page. He will not respond to that headline because the headline does not ask him to probe deeper into the ad. If we added a benefit to that headline it would read like this: 'We'll Show You How To Make Money The Easy Way'. Here are more examples of good headlines: 'Save $50' or 'Buy Quality Books At A Discount'. Another type of headline that is effective is one that contains a benefit but also asks the reader a question. The curiosity of your prospect moves him to read the ad. Here are some examples of this type of headline: 'Would You Like To Become Rich?', 'How Would You Like To Make Big Money?' and 'Are You Tired Of Low Wages?'. Yet another way to catch a reader is to write a headline that arouses his attention. Here are some examples of this type of headline: 'Free Money', 'My Money Secrets' and 'Becoming Rich'.

Getting Good At Writing Headlines

If you are still not sure how to write headlines like the ones shown, then study the headlines in mail order magazines or newspapers. Make sure the ad appears quite a few times in order to make sure it was successful. To get a good feel for good and bad ads, start a portfolio of ads. If you see an ad in a publication that you like, cut it out and put the ad in a "like" file. If you see an ad that you don't like, cut it out and put it in a "dislike" file. When you study your ads you will be able to find out what makes a good ad good and what makes a bad one bad.

Words That Appeal To Your Audience

When certain words are contained in a headline, the headline becomes more effective. If you add at least one of the following words to your headline it becomes more appealing to your readers. Notice how often you will find them in your "like" file. They include: FREE, GUARANTEE, SAVE, DISCOUNT, MONEY, MAKE MONEY, EASY, PROFIT, PROSPER, SECRET, SPECIAL, NOW, YOU, ANNOUNCING, INTRO-DUCING, MODERN, NEW, LOW COST, ADVICE TO..., HOW TO..., WHY, GET VALUE, WHOLE-SALE, SOLUTION, SALE, SENSATIONAL & AMAZING.

Writing Your Subhead

The subhead is located just below the headline in smaller type. Its main purpose is to expand on the headline. The subhead is written the same way as the headline. It is just an expanded form of the headline. An example of this is:

GOLD JEWELRY
Your Quick Way to Make Easy Money

Get Into Big Profit Sales
You Will Get Moneymaking Benefits
Work Part or Full Time
Free Booklet

A lot of the time the sub-headlines are scattered all over the page. In this way, the advertiser is hoping that one of his headlines will interest you to read the ad.

Capturing Your Target Audience

If you want to get a certain audience to read your ad then you must use a headline to capture your audience and a subhead to tell your readers of the benefits of your products or service. Here are examples of this type of ad:

A)   **PET OWNERS**
B)   Save Money With This New Flea Collar

Headline (A) catches the attention of all pet owners. Anyone that owns a pet will notice the ad. Sub-headline (B) tells the reader exactly what you are going to do for him (i.e., save him money on flea collars).

Writing Body Copy That Sells

The body copy is the complete copy of your ad. Your body copy (the middle of your ad) convinces your readers to respond to your offer. The following guidelines should be followed when writing your body copy and your headline.

Preparing To Write Your Copy

When writing copy the first thing you should do is make a list of all the benefits of your product or service. Elaborate on each individual benefit as much as you can. After you have completed the list, number the benefits and review them for accuracy. Start to write your copy using all of the benefits you have listed on your sheet. With this simple technique you will be able to write remarkable copy.

Reader Benefit

Explain to your prospect clearly and plainly how he or she can benefit from buying your product or service.

The "You" Attitude

Write all of your copy with a "You" attitude. This makes your readers feel that you are interested in them and not in yourself. Here are some examples of a few sentence with and without this point of view:

(without)   Earn up to $50
(with)   You can earn up to $50

(without)   I can make dreams come true
(with)   I can make all your dreams come true.

If you read through enough advertising copy, you will find that the best ones contain the "You" attitude.

Positive Atmosphere

Don't say anything negative in your ad. Never tell people what you can't do, always tell them what you *can* do. There is a positive side to every circumstance. If you sold a product and you only had red and blue but not yellow and green, you don't tell your prospects that you don't have yellow and green, you tell them that you do have blue and red. Here is an example of a corrected statement. "You shouldn't be poor" becomes "You should be rich."

Present Tense

Studies have shown that the present tense has the best selling impact, therefore, you should use it.

Captions Under Illustrations

If you have any illustrations or pictures in your ads, put captions under them. Captions under illustrations get a high readership. Putting a brief message under each caption will pay off.

Simplify Your Writing

It is good practice to avoid long sentences when writing ads. You want to make your ads as easy as possible for your readers to read and understand. Your sentences should not have more than 20 words.

What Words To Use

You want to make sure that the words you use in your ads are understood by your readers. Even if they are understood by your readers you want to make sure it doesn't take your readers too long to digest your message. Communicate with your readers in familiar words. Here are some examples of difficult words converted into easy-to-understand words: utilize—use, ascertain—find out, substantial—a great deal. If you have to use two or three words to substitute for a harder-to-understand-word, then do it.

How To Test Your Ad For Clarity

If you want the majority of people to read and comprehend your ad very well then you must state your ideas in simple form. Your writing should be at the seventh grade level. If you are not sure your writing can be read and understood with ease, try this. Get an average 12-year-old to read your ad. Make sure he can read and understand your ad easily and clearly.

Give Free Information

One way to get an excellent response from your ad is to give out free information. Free information arouses curiosity and it also prompts the reader to respond to your ad because he has nothing to lose. You must arrange for the ''free information'' to come first and the sales talk to come second in order to get the most from your ad.

Use Long Copy

Talk about your product or service as much as you can. As a general rule, the more copy you have, the more prospects you get. If you want immediate sales, you need a complete, long selling message.

Make Your Copy Dynamic

Start off by writing a great deal on your topic. Write a lot more than you will use for your final ad. After you have done this, edit your writing. Keep only the portions of your copy that you feel are important. Your copy will greatly improve in quality after it is edited down. This is the way great copy writers write ads. If you want to be of that caliber, use this technique.

Create a Demand For Your Product

If I got more people to buy soda, then I have increased the primary demand for soft drinks. If you were the Coca-Cola Company, you would want people to buy just your cola, not all colas. When you write your ad, make sure you are not helping your competition advertise. Advertise only your company, your product and your service.

Ending Your Copy

Every good advertiser knows that when you end your copy you must get your reader to act. Your ultimate goal is to get action. What better time to do it than after you have finished your sales talk? Tell your reader what to do to "make his life better." One of the best ways to get immediate action is to give the reader a good reason for responding immediately, such as: the price is going up, supplies are limited, a bonus offer, a time limit on the offer.

Giving Your Ad The Professional Touch

After you have written your headline, sub-headlines and body copy, you should complete your ad by placing your logo at the bottom. It should consist of your name, address and a special symbol identifying your company. For more information on logos, look under the section, "Creating A Distinct Company Image."

How To Stimulate Responses To Get Quick Results

Try to offer an inexpensive but attractive gift if your prospect orders within a certain time frame, (i.e., 10 days). This increases sales because this method gets your prospects who procrastinate to respond quicker to your ad. You will get more results if you include a coupon with your sales literature or ad. Anything that makes ordering more convenient for your prospect will get you a quicker response. *Reader's Digest* includes a pencil with its subscription renewals so you don't have to run around the house looking for something to write with. When using direct mail literature you can speed responses by using a self addressed envelope. You can further increase your responses by using return-business-reply envelopes. With this type of envelope you pay twice the postage for the envelopes that reach you. It is still worth the response at twice the rate. Check with your nearest post office for more information.

If you would like more details on the money-raising tricks and gimmicks that so many use in the mail order business, you might consider looking at a book called "How To

Make A Fortune From Direct Mail" by George Strong. It is available through Lion Publishing Co. for just $15.00. You can order a copy by writing to them at 6150 Mission Gorge Rd., San Diego, Calif, 92120.

Getting An Advertising Discount

It is possible to get a 15% discount on all the advertising you place. Advertising agencies charge you for placing an ad and then they collect a 15% commission on your ad. They use the 15% for preparing and placing your ad. All you have to do to get this 15% discount is to tell the magazine or newspaper that you operate an in-house advertising agency. These next few steps will benefit you if you are contemplating getting your 15% advertising discount. Be sure that you can write good ads. If you can't write good ads, you may lose more that the 15% you have saved. Most advertising agencies know what they are doing, which is why they get the 15% reduction. If you would like to collect the 15% commission and have a good ad, follow this advice. Follow all of my suggestions and create an ad according to my directions. Then take the rough lay-out to a professional to prepare your ad for you.

Increase Your Advertising Knowledge

The more books on advertising you study, the better you will be at writing ads. One book I especially recommend is "How To Write A Good Advertisement, A Short Course In Copywriting", by Victor O. Schwab, one of the best copywriters of this century. He created many famous ads—one ad for "How To Win Friends And Influence People", sold 5 million copies for author Dale Carnegie.

Schwab's techniques are continually studied by the top advertising agencies, and you should study them, too. Instead of focusing on the structure of the successful ad, Schwab concentrates on the psychology of the consumer. If you know what consumers want and need, your ads will do very well. After reading this book, you should be able to pin-point the precise needs of your customers and know how to fulfill them. You can pick up this 227-page, 8½ x 11-inch book at most fine book stores for $16. If you have trouble finding it, I can ship it to you within 48 hours for only $16, including postage and insurance. Just write to: Lion Publishing Co., 6150 Mission Gorge Road, Suite 225, San Diego, CA 92120.

Be An Advertising Executive Just From Watching TV

Ten years ago, households with cable television were few and far between. As the 1990's approach, however, it is estimated that nearly 39% or all American households with a television set will have it tuned to a cable network channel. Cable TV is big money these days, and if you have your own business, it can bring in the big money for you.

Many cable stations use much more flexible advertising format than do the established networks, and many small businesses are capitalizing on these innovative types of television commercials. Perhaps you have seen them, and maybe you were not even aware that you were looking at an advertisement. Some are in the form of documentary or informational shows, some look like talk shows, still others are made to resemble auctions or warehouse sales.

If your business sells a product or service that would lend itself to this type of advertisement, you may be able to attract a larger market audience by contracting the services of a marketing company. These companies are experts in marketing and advertising on these cable networks, and they will determine the best marketing strategy for your product. Their fee comes from a percentage of your increased sales and profits, and often there is no initial capital outlay. Some of these agencies will even take a sample of your product and manufacture it for you.

To find out what type of product would sell well in your area through cable TV advertising, contact a marketing company in near you. If you want more information on this type of advertising, let me recommend an excellent book on the subject. It is called **$1,000,000 Cash Vision,** and is available from Lion Publishing Co., 6150 Mission Gorge Rd., Suite 225, San Diego, CA 92120. The cost is just $12.95.

Making Big Money With Your Telephone

For those people interested in competing in the business world, and more specifically in marketing, anything that you can do to increase your potential sales is considered good business. **One way to do this is by acquiring an 800 number.** Offering a toll-free number to potential clients gives them added incentive to call you for more information because they know they won't be billed for the call. Once you get that potential client on the phone, a salesman can speak with them and persuade the client to purchase the product or service they were inquiring about.

If you are selling a product through a brochure, it is to your advantage to include an 800 number. That way, the potential client has a chance to see the product (if you include a photo) and call immediately if he is interested. If your potential client is intrigued enough to make that call, a good salesman will probably be able to convince him to buy. Since the most expensive products are sold person to person, a salesman can sell much better than just a brochure. An 800 number will enable you to provide specialized information which would otherwise be very difficult to convey.

You can also pitch your product to a targeted audience. All you do is promote the 800 number to the people who you feel fall into this category and if they're interested they'll call in. The cost of each call to you is approximately 22 cents per minute, depending on where the call is coming from. When setting up an 800 number, it is best to go through a carrier such as MCI as opposed to AT&T. o7 3

The response rate is much higher with an 800 number. By using an 800 number, your response is 10 to 20 percent of your target audience, as opposed to advertising through a magazine with a display ad, which has an average response of only .5 percent of your target audience.

Selling a product or service over the phone is one of the most profitable ways of marketing available today and offering an 800 number simplifies and facilitates the process. With an 800 number, you can persuade the potential client to purchase your product, take his Visa or Mastercard number, mail the product immediately, and leave the burden of collection to the credit agency. The easier you make it for people to order a product or service without creating a hassle, (added hassles include writing a check and putting a stamp on the envelope, etc...) the more likely they are going to order the product or service you are offering.

Getting Free Publicity

Who Gets Free Publicity

Almost all publications accept publicity. The criteria for free publicity is the same for all publications. If your product or service is unique and different, then you have a good chance at getting free publicity. The reason publications give out free publicity is so that their customers can get a new and different product or service. It is done for the convenience of the customer and it adds interest to the magazine. When the pet rock came out, the promoters of that idea didn't pay one cent for advertising. The pet rock was new, different and amused people. Hundreds of publications published stories on the pet rock from news releases and interviews. If your product or service isn't unique and different, make it unique and different. Many times, if you buy an ad from magazines, they will give you a free editorial.

How To Get Free Publicity

An editorial is an article written about your product. Getting an editorial written about your product and having a picture of your product in a magazine is like getting a free display ad. In many cases you will get a better response from an editorial than from a paid ad. The reason for this is that an editorial will have more credibility than an ordinary display ad. If you make it convenient for a magazine or a newspaper to write an editorial for you then your chances of getting the editorial are much greater. The best way to get an editorial is to submit a press release, a letter to the editor and a picture of your product to the publication of your choice. We are going to show you how to prepare your publicity materials.

Writing A Press Release

When writing a press release, the first thing you should do is make a list of all of the benefits of you product or service. Elaborate on each individual benefit as much as you can. After you have completed the list, number the benefits and review your paper for accuracy. Start to write your press release using all of the best benefits you have listed on your benefit sheet. You will find that you will be able to write remarkable copy with this simple technique. Also, use the same principles used for writing advertising copy with some exceptions listed below.

The Third Person Point Of View

When you write a press release you must make it seem as if you are a magazine observing your own company. You must write your editorials in the third person. Here is an example of editorial style: Instead of 'We will send you a book,' use 'They will send you a book.' Instead of 'Write today for free details,' use 'Write Smith Enterprises today for free details.'

News Style

When you write a press release you are not trying to promote yourself, you are trying to educate people through news. You must write in a factual news style of writing. You must imagine yourself as a reporter doing an interview on the product or service. We have enclosed examples of the news release and the letter to the editor for your benefit.

NEWS RELEASE

From: Smith Enterprises
786 Broadway St.
New York, NY 11235

For Immediate Release
Beat Las Vegas At Its Own Game

Do you want to beat Las Vegas at its own game? Smith Enterprises can help you do just that. They have a unique book that outlines systems used by professionals in the casinos. The systems in their book are easy to learn and anyone can use them. Their blackjack systems are created by a computer.

Your Photograph

In order for the publishers to show a picture of your product in their publication you must send a black-and-white picture. Get a glossy print or a picture of your product from the manufacturer, and have it reproduced. Most places ask for photographs that are 8 x 10 inches. Send the magazine a 4 x 5 inch photograph instead. The smaller size is adequate with the magazines and mail-order houses. Also, you will save on postage and reproduction costs with the smaller photograph.

Who Will Give You Publicity?

Certain magazines will give you more publicity than others. Your problem is finding out which magazines are the best to write to. I am going to make that task easy for you. To get a list of magazines that will accept publicity releases, go to your nearest library or book store and find "Bacon's Publicity Checker for Consumer Magazines." It lists almost all the magazines that accept publicity releases. The book "Consumer Magazine and Farm Publications Rates and Data" has a list of 300 magazines carrying mail-order shopping sections suitable for publicity. Your best bet out of the two books mentioned is "Bacon's Publicity Checker." If you are having a hard time getting the names of magazines which will accept publicity, then the following service will help you. Lion Publishing Co. is selling fresh names of magazines that are accepting publicity. These names were carefully selected to include only the names of magazines anxious to give products free publicity. All the names and addresses of the magazines are reliable and come on self- stick pressure-sensitive labels. You can buy 250 names for only $35. If you would like to receive them, write Lion Publishing Co., 6150 Mission Gorge Road, Suite 225, San Diego, CA 92120.

Lion Publishing Co. also sells a book entirely devoted to the subject of publicity advertising titled, **"Getting Free Publicity"** by Samuel Wood. It is available for only $15.

A Direct Mail Overview

What Is Direct Mail Advertising?

For the professional mail-order dealer, direct mail is an important and powerful strategy. Direct mail is a form of advertising that involves sending your sales material directly to your prospective customer and is made possible by the rental of lists of names from others or by special mailings to your own house list of customers and prospects. Planning and preparation are essential in a direct-mail campaign. The following are some of the essential elements that you'll need to know in order to achieve success using direct mail.

If you would like more details on any of these strategies, I suggest you get a copy of **"How To Make A Fortune From Direct Mail"** from Lion Publishing Co., at 6150 Mission Gorge Rd., #225, San Diego, CA, 92120. The cost is $15.00.

The Benefits Of Direct Mail

Direct mail advertising is one of the most successful means available of reaching a desired audience. There are many reasons why buyers are attracted to products and services that are advertised and sold by mail. For instance, something offered by mail usually offers a bargain to the consumer. Or perhaps the buyer doesn't wish to meet with a salesman face-to-face, either out of embarrassment or fear of giving in under pressure. Mail- order offers the consumer convenience by letting him shop from his own home, and sometimes having a product arrive through the mail gives the buyer a feeling of adventure. More than ever, mail-order direct-mail marketing is a successful means of advertising.

The Five Major Advantages Of Direct Mail

Direct mail is perhaps the most efficient way of reaching your desired audience. By recognizing and adapting the five major advantages of direct mail, you can better understand how to use this unique and powerful tool. Those advantages are:

1) Accurately reaching your desired market.
2) Personalization.
3) Speed in getting to the market.
4) Concealment of test information.
5) More sales copy possible.

Accurately Reaching Your Desired Market

The first major advantage of direct mail is the ability to define and locate your market accurately. With this approach you can tune in precisely to your targeted market through the rental of the name list that you use. Are you interested in selling your product to women executives? List brokers offer breakdowns in the category of women executives by age, income, and job functions; whether divorced, single, widowed, or married; special classifications of women executives can even be compiled by religion, social organizations, high school and college graduates, occupation, and so on. You simply can't reach this degree of market accuracy when using classified or display advertisements in magazines or newspapers.

Personalization

The second major advantage is the personalized approach. You can tailor your mailing piece directly to your potential customer. If you have a computer, you can address each direct mailing piece to the individual that you're trying to reach. It is this personalized feature of direct mail that helps to make it a winner. Direct mail works equally well whether you are selling a product, a service, or yourself.

Speed In Getting To The Market

Speed is one of the greatest advantages of direct mail. If you wish to advertise in a magazine, the lead item for placing your ad could be up to six weeks or more; and then you must wait up to a full year before you receive most of your responses. With direct mail your waiting time is practically nil. You can mail whenever you're ready. By using direct mail, you will receive half your response only one week after the first inquiry! This means that you will know at once whether your proposition is profitable or not. If it is, you can expand your promotion with no lead time. Furthermore, you will receive all your responses six months after receiving the first inquiry and you will have 95% after only two months. If mail order has the potential of being a fast way to riches, the direct mail method has the potential of being super fast.

Concealment Of Test Information

Maintaining confidentiality of your operations is very important in mail-order because it is easy for potential competitors to see what you are doing. With display or even classified advertising, it's impossible to conceal success at all. Your success can be spotted easily by your repeated advertising. Direct mail is also open to your competitors since many names on a list will be individuals who are interested or engaged in mail-order operations. However, your competition can't track everything that you're doing since it is unlikely that any one competitor will see more than a small portion of your mailings to different lists. Because you're being able to keep much of your advertising confidential (except to the individuals who receive the ads), it is also easier to test various prices with little chance of confusing or irritating your potential customers. Although not a major problem, it is true that if you take a full-page display ad that indicates one price, it is difficult to show the same display ad in another magazine at another price without creating some confusing and questions in the minds of your prospective customers. With direct mail, you can test many different prices with a reduced chance that the same potential customer will see many of your different prices being tested.

More Sales Copy Possible

The best advantage is the extra space that you have for your sales pitch. If you were to advertise in magazines or newspapers, you would be limited to a single-page display ad, or to a few words in a classified. But this is not so with direct mail! Your direct mail package could include a multi-page letter, a flier, an order blank, testimonials, and a guarantee card. In fact, your letter to a customer may go from four to six pages by itself. As a consequence, you have a much greater chance of making the sale than if less copy was necessitated by limitations of space and cost in a magazine. All of these things, which are detailed further, will give you a much better opportunity to promote what you're selling.

What Kind Of Profit You Can Expect

It is important to understand the economics of direct mail. An industry rule of thumb is that a product of wide interest that is advertised to an average-buying audience will produce a 1.5% to 2% response. In other words, for every 1,000 pieces, 15 to 20 orders: for every 10,000, 150 to 200, etc.

To do well in direct mail, your campaign should bring in orders totaling 2.2 times what the campaign cost you. For example, if your campaign cost $1,000, you should bring in $2,200 to justify your time and effort. However, your bottom line should always be the total number of dollars that you can make. Profits, not percentages, should be your main concern.

The Seven Basic Types of Direct Mail Offers

Here is a listing of the basics that your offer might contain and a breakdown of each item:

1) Offering the product at the right price.
2) Trial Periods.
3) Money-back guarantees.
4) Billing options.
5) Free offers.
6) Discounts and sales.
7) Acting in a timely fashion.

Offering The Product At The Right Price

When creating your offer, setting the right price for your product can be a very gray item to address. The right price will depend on what the market dictates at any given moment. If you price your product too low, people might think it is not worthy of purchase. Of course, if you set the price too high you take the chance of pricing yourself out of the market. A good rule of thumb is to check out your competition to see what they are charging for their products, than adapt your offer accordingly. However, you should also keep in mind what it will take for your product to make a profit. It will do you no good to undersell a competitor if the cost means cutting your own throat.

Trial Periods

In this day and age of mail-order marketing, it is no longer an option for you to offer a free trial period in your advertisement. It is a necessity. Again, look to your competition to see what offers are being made and for how long. Most offers will allow a 10 to 14 day trial period, but others will allow a month or more.

Money-Back Guarantees

A money-back guarantee is the cornerstone to any successful direct-mail campaign. Consumers do take a risk by sending their money to an unknown source and buying something unseen. So in order to persuade buyers, a guarantee must be made to insure satisfaction. This is usually stated with "Money Back Guarantee If You're Not Completely Satisfied" or some other similar statement. Some manufacturers are so insistent that you'll love their product that they even offer a "double-your-money back guarantee", thus putting the manufacturer at a gamble for the customer's satisfaction. However, the person making the offer will always have an added advantage over the consumer, because of the time and inconvenience of sending a product back. A good formula to gauge your success is to tabulate your returns and see if they make less than 15% of your sales. If they do, then your campaign should be a success. If your returns are more than 15% of your orders, you may want to reevaluate your product, your service, or your advertising claims.

Billing Options

There are essentially five options that the mail-order dealer has when collecting money for his product:

1) Check or Money Orders. Most offers will use this basic form of payment, which is to simply include a check or money order with your order. The sending of cash through the mail is not recommended, because it leaves no record of accountability should an order become lost in the mail or incorrectly handled in some fashion.

2) Free-Trial Period. If you are offering a free-trial period for your product, most companies will bill you when the merchandise is delivered. This is a popular form of doing business, and your response will be much greater than if you had required payment with the order. However, there is the inevitable problem of people not paying you, or refusing to return your product. If the percentage of people who do this doesn't kill your profit margin, then you should consider this a natural by-product of offering a product with a trial period

3) Installment Plan. If you are offering a product with a high price tag, a good way of inducing a customer to buy is to allow him to pay you in installments.

4) Credit Card. This is probably the most desirable form of payment because it puts the burden of collection on the credit card company and not on you. There is, of course, a percentage that the credit card company will assess for its services, but it is generally low enough for this to be an attractive form of payment.

Free Offers

Offering a free gift is an excellent way to get a customer's attention and get him to act immediately to your sales pitch. If you choose to offer a free gift, you will want to tie it in somehow to what it is that you're offering. It won't make much sense to offer a free tie pin if you're selling something that doesn't have to do with ties. Also, you will receive a certain amount of requests from people who just want to receive the free gift, so include a statement such as "please include 50 cents for handling" to weed out those who are simply curiosity seekers.

Discounts And Sales

Discount offers have an appeal because buyers are always looking for a bargain. Many companies will offer their products at a discount, hoping that by enticing you with a bargain on one item, you'll be satisfied and want to but more at the full price. Some companies will offer a refund, sending you a check with your discount after you have bought and used the product.

Sales tend to be offered seasonally, such as on Labor Day, Memorial Day, or Christmas. A company may be forced into offering a sale due to circumstances beyond their control, such as a fire, inventory clearance, or going out of business. Sometimes stating that a price increase will be occurring soon is a good way of getting people interested in your product. **Whatever the reason, you should always state why you are having a sale.**

Acting In A Timely Fashion

Tied in with sample offers, discount, and sales, is a time limit for the special being offered. It is important to have the customer act in as timely a fashion as possible, so that other offers can be made to him. Products that are offered for a ''limited time only'', spark interest and induce the customer to act immediately.

If you would like to market your product through direct mail, you may be interested in National Publications' six book series entitled Direct Response Millions. For information concerning the series, please call: (619) 280-5050.

How To Save Money
On Printing And Mailing

Saving on Mailings

1) If you mail more than 200 pieces of the same mail all at once, try using the bulk rate. If every mailing piece is the same size and you are willing to sort the mail in zip codes, you can get the bulk rate. It costs $50 a year for the necessary permit to get the bulk rate, and you only pay 12.5 cents per mailing piece up to four ounces. Check with your local post office for more details.

2) Use a scale to find your needed postage, and regularly check the scale. You can check your scales by weighing nine pennies; they should weigh one ounce.

3) When you are mailing books, use the special fourth class book rate; it is 69 cents per pound for the first pound, 25 cents per pound for pounds two through seven, and 15 cents per pound for 8 pounds up through the limit of 70 pounds.

4) Mail other mail-order circulars with your own circulars. You can save a great deal in postage and you can even make a profit.

5) Pay a company to mail your circulars with theirs. Many companies advertise this service. If you can't find a company that will do this, write mail-order companies asking them if they do. They will charge you about 4 cents per circular to mail the circular to their customers.

How To Save Money On Printing

1) Use a high-grade, light-weight paper instead of a lower-grade, heavier-weight paper.

2) If you want to get the effect of three-color printing at a low cost, print colored ink on two-colored paper.

3) Before having a printer do any work for you, ask him for samples of other printing he has done in the past. Some printers have inferior machines that create cheap, blurry copies.

4) Have your copy ready for the printer to photograph (called camera-ready copy). If you have your copy in this form you will save money. There is no extra charge for enlarging or shrinking your copy. Your copy must be pure black or red on white paper. In most cases, even if the paper is colored, the printer can shoot the copy. Check with your printer. You can use a light blue to write on your copy and it will not show up when your copy is printed. Do not erase on the original copy since light blue is invisible to the printer's camera. You can use liquid paper to take out dirt, smudges and anything else that you don't want printed. Leave a ¼ inch margin on anything printed, so that the printing machine can grab the paper. Get all of your pictures made into half tones. Half tones are little dots that make up the picture. If you look at a printed picture with a magnifying glass, you will be able to see them. It costs about $4 to get a half tone done. You can get them done cheaper with a Xerox machine but the quality won't be as good. The camera will only pick up what it sees. A clean and neat original will produce neat, ciear copies.

Money From Your Importing Business

Many small importation businesses have started up in the last few years. This type of money-making venture is very easy to get into and simple to maintain, all it takes is a little marketing know-how and the advertising abilities you have gained by reading this book.

Some people fear that they cannot enter into the imports business for lack of money, but nothing could be further from the truth. In a drop-ship business, your customers give you cash for the merchandise and your suppliers ship the goods directly to the customer. You never touch the shipments, just make a trip to the bank.

To begin, you must contact a supplier who manufactures a product or product line that you are interested in selling. Pick something you have a little knowledge in or are interested in learning about. Nearly every product you can imagine is manufactured overseas, although you might stay away from items that are very delicate and might break in shipping, or items which are more expensive, and therefore more difficult to sell in bulk. Quantity is your main goal! An excellent source of suppliers is the **"Drop Shipping Directory"**, which is available from National Publications for just $15. You can order it from them at 6150 Mission Gorge Rd., #225, San Diego, CA, 92120.

When you have discovered some type of ware that you find unique or saleable in some way, then you must find a market for it. Check with local small businesses, nik-nack stores, your friends and relatives, and advertise in local magazines and newspapers. You will be amazed at how much interest will be generated when people find out how inexpensively they can purchase these interesting items.

Once you have spread the word about the unique items you are offering for sale, people will seek you out to purchase these goods. All you need to do is to take their name, address, and money. After you have collected the minimum amount required for an order, print each customer's name and address on a shipping label and send it to your supplier along with the payment for the goods. They will drop-ship the merchandise directly to your customers and your business will be concluded. You will soon find that your friends and clients are so amazed at the bargains that they have received that they will come to you again and again.

Before setting up this type of business, you will want to contact the Federal Government to assure yourself that you are complying with all laws and regulations. They can furnish you with all the information you need to start your business.

A superb publication concerning the business of drop shipping is **How You Can Make Millions In The Import/Export Market.** The cost is $29.95, and it is available from Lion Publishing Co., 6150 Mission Gorge Rd., Suite 225, San Diego, CA 92120.

FOREIGN DROP-SHIP SUPPLIERS

APPLIANCES

Saramac Limited, Sanyo Bldg., 23-28, Edobori 1 chome, Nishi-ku, Osaka 550, Japan.

Li Fong Industrial Co., Ltd., P.O.Box 68—145, Taipei, Taiwan, R.O.C.

ART OBJECTS

Setsco Pte Ltd., 179 River Valley Road, Singapore-0617.

New Spring Trading Co., Ltd., P.O.Box 1079, Taipei, Taiwan, R.O.C.

CALCULATORS

Dah Sun Electronics Co. Ltd., P.O. Box 98712 T.S.T., Hong Kong

CAMERAS

Farsharp Industrial Corp. 10/F-4, 1010, Ming Sheng E. Rd., Taipei, Taiwan, R.O.C.; P.O. Box 87-354 Taipei, Taiwan

Kingmark Hitco Taiwan Ltd., 11th Fl.-1, No. 103, Sec. 4, Nanking E. Rd., Paipei, Taiwan, R.O.C.; Mailing Address: P.O. Box 81-865, Taipei, Taiwan, R.O.C.

San Ping Enterprise Co., Ltd., 5th Fl., Pai Hwei Building, No. 32, Teh Hwei St., Taipei, Taiwan, R.O.C.

CLOCKS

Mustard Int'l. Co., Ltd., P.O. Box 68-1402, Taipei, Taiwan, R.O.C.

High-Dome Industrial Co., Ltd., P.O. Box 24-225, Taipei, Taiwan.

Verobel International Corp., Export Dept., P.O. Box 334, 3430 AH Nieuwegein, The Netherlands

ART OBJECTS

Western Graphics Corporation, 2608 S.E. Gladstone, Portland, Oregon, 97202, U.S.A.

Setsco Pte. Ltd., 179 River Valley Rd., Singapore-0617.

CLOTHING

Pore International Inc., 4th Fl.-2, -3, No. 99, Fu Hsing N. Rd.,
Taipei, Taiwan, R.O.C.

Pehpeng Enterprise Co., Ltd., 1-5, Kou Hu Tzu, Chung Liao Li, Tan Shui Chen, Taipei Hsien, Taiwan, R.O.C.

Hsin Hou Hsing Enterprise Co., Ltd., No. 203, Sec. 2, Chin Hua Rd., Tainan, Taiwan, R.O.C.

Ming Tai Enterprises Co., Ltd., 114, Mei Luen St., Shih Lin District, Taipei, Taiwan, R.O.C.

COSMETICS AND PERFUME

Jung Hua Cosmetics Co., Ltd., No. 1, Hsin Chung Rd., Anping Industrial Dist., Tainan, Taiwan, R.O.C.

Mei Shual Cosmetics Co., Ltd., P.O. Box 13-45, Tainan, Taiwan, R.O.C.

Wei Mei Li Chemical Mfg. Co., Ltd., 5th Fl.-1, No. 112, Chung Hsiao E. Rd., Sec. 4, Taipei, Taiwan, R.O.C.

SHOES

Keh Jye Corporation, 1Fl., 32, Min Chuan Rd., Yung Ho, Taipei Hsien, Taiwan, R.O.C.

Ry-Co International Ltd., 4F, 624, Min Chuan E. Rd., Taipei, Taiwan, R.O.C.

GEMS AND STONES

Harvest-Jen Enterprise Co., Ltd., No. 23, Kuei Lin Rd., Taipei, Taiwan, R.O.C.

Jamie Gem Stone Manufacturing Co., Ltd., 10 Fl., No. 164, Sec. 4, Nan King E. Rd., Taipei, Taiwan, R.O.C.

GENERAL MERCHANDISE

Kou Tern Trade Co., Ltd., P.O. Box 1266 Taichung, Taiwan.

Industrias Cervello S.a., Marques de Sentmenat, 12 Barcelona-14, Spain

GIFT ITEMS

Taiwan General Co. Ltd., P.O. Box 72-66, Taipei, Taiwan

Everbest and Co., G.P.O. Box 9086, Hog Kong

Andreas Klemm, 6 Wernerwerkstrasse, D-8400 Regensburg, West Germany

HAIR GOODS

Po Go Industrial Co., Ltd., P.O. Box 394, Feng Yuan, Taiwan, R.O.C.

HANDBAGS

Ynh Fonz Enterprise Co., Ltd., 612, Yung Fu Rd., Chung Li, Tao Yuan Hsien, Taiwan, R.O.C.

Ching Chi Plastics Baggage Co., Ltd., 256, San Min District, Ta Lien Str, Kaohsiung, Taiwan, R.O.C.

HANDICRAFTS

Kemperling Kg, A-5136 Mattsee/Salzburg, Austria, Europe.

JEWELRY

Shapton Industrial Corp., P.O. Box 84-196, Taipei, Taiwan

Staf Corporation, C.P.O. Box 6010 Seoul, Korea.

NOVELTIES

Preissler GmbH, Emma-Jager Str. 1,7530 Pforzheim, West-Germany

PAINTINGS AND PICTURES

Kwang-Yuh Art Co., LTD., P.O. Box 1769, Kaohsiung, Taiwan

RADIOS

Chiefly Faith Co., LTD., P.O. Box 1917, Taipei, Taiwan

TOOLS

Birdland Industries Inc., P.O. Box 53-245, Taipei, Taiwan, R.O.C.

Maglake Industrial Co., Ltd., P.O. Box 427, Kaohsiung, Taiwan.

WATCHES

Adolf Hanhart Uhren Fabrik GmbH and Co Kg., D-7730 Villingen Schwenningen, Postfach 3247, West Germany

Erwen Schlup, Herwins-Ufesa, CH-2543 Lengnau/Biel, Switzerland

How U.S. Government Will Lend You $15,000 Without Collateral

The U.S. Small Business Administration will provide capital to start a worthy small new business at reasonable terms. Loans range from $200 to $100,000-and this financing opportunity is available to anyone wanting to start a new small business up to $15,000 on the basis of a GOOD REPUTATION only—with NO collateral needed. Get complete FREE information from the nearest U.S. Small Business Administration Office. Write: SBA, 1441 L St., NW. Washington DC 20416. They can send you the loan application. (202) 653-6881. Lion Publishing also puts out two books on the subject titled "Cashing In On Government Money" which sells for $12.95, and "Getting The Government To Pay For Your New Business" which costs $14.95. For more information write: Lion Publishing Co., 6150 Mission Gorge Road, Suite 225, San Diego, CA 92120.

Free Grants and Low-Interest Loans

If you need money to finance your business venture, there is one book I recommend: **"The Complete Guide To Getting Free Grants and Low-Interest Loans."** It is truly unique because it is one of the only guides with about 500 institutions that give out or loan low-interest money. The book is guaranteed to get you the money you need. In fact, some of the programs which the book offers require you to have bad credit to qualify. This book is only $12.00, postage paid. It is available from Federated Financial Services, Suite 300, 5515 Jackson, Dept. SO-3, La Mesa, CA 92041.

VENTURE CAPITAL SOURCES

Adler and Company
375 Park Avenue
New York, NY 10152

Advanced Technology Ventures
1000 El Camino Real
Menlo Park, CA 94025

R.W. Allsop & Associates
2750 First Ave., N.E.
Cedar Rapids, IA 52402

Broventure Company, Inc.
16 W. Madison St
Baltimore, MD 21201

Bryan and Edwards
3000 San Hill Rd.
Menlo Park, CA 94025

Allstate Insurance Company
Allstate Plaza, Blvd. E-2
Northbrook, IL 60062

American Research & Development
45 Milk St.
Boston, MA 02109

Faneuil Hall Associates
1 Boston Place
Boston, MA 02108

Asset Management Company
2275 E. Bayshore Rd.
Palo Alto, CA 94303

Brentwood Associates
11661 San Vicente Blvd.
Los Angeles, CA 90049

InnoVen Group
Park 80 Plaza West-One
Saddle Brook, NJ 07662

Institutional Venture Associates
3000 San Hill Rd., Bldg. 2
Menlo Park, CA 94025

Burr, Egan, Delage & Co., Inc.
One Post Office Sq.
Boston, MA 02109

Cable, Howse & Cozadd, Inc.
777 108th St.
Bellevue, WA 98004

Capital Southwest Corporation
12900 Preston Rd.
Dallas, TX 75230

Charles River Partnership
67 Battery March St.
Boston, MA 02110

Citicorp Venture Capital Ltd.
153 E. 53rd
New York, NY 10043

Colorado Growth Capital, Inc.
1600 Broadway
Denver, CO 80202

Continental Capital Ventures
555 California Street
San Francisco, CA 94104

Continental Illinois Venture
231 S. LaSalle St.
Chicago, IL 60697

Curtin & Company, Inc.
2050 Houston Natural Gas Bldg.
Houston, TX 77002

Fidelity Venture Associates
82 Devonshire St.
Boston, MA 02109

First Century Partnership II
1345 Avenue of the Americas
New York, NY 10105

First Interstate Venture Capital, Inc.
5000 Birch St.
Newport Beach, CA 92660

First Midwest Capital Corp.
15 South Fifth Street
Minneapolis, MN 55402

Foster Management Company
437 Madison Ave.
New York, NY 10022

Frontenac Company
208 So. LaSalle Street
Chicago, IL 60604

Golder, Thomas & Co.
120 S. LaSalle Street
Chicago, IL 60604

Greylock Management Corporation
One Federal Street
Boston, MA 02110

Hambrecht & Quist
235 Montgomery Street
San Francisco, CA 94104

Harvest Ventures, Inc.
767 3rd
New York, NY 10117

Intercapco, Inc
7800 Bon Homme Ave
St. Louis, MO 63105

Interwest Partners
3000 Sandhill Rd.
Menlo Park, CA 94025

J.H. Whitney & Company
630 Fifth Ave.
New York, NY 10111

Kleiner Perkins Caulfield & Buyers
Four Embarcadero Center
San Francisco, CA 94111

Lawrence, WPG Partners L.P.
515 Madison Ave
New York, NY 10022

Lubrizol Enterprises, Inc.
29400 Lakeland Boulevard
Wickliffe, OH 44092

Mayfield III
2200 San Hill Road
Menlo Park, CA 94025

Memorial Drive Trust
20 Acorn Park
Cambridge, MA 02140

Menlo Ventures
3000 San Hill Rd.
Menlo Park, CA 94025

Merrill, Pickard Capital Co.
Two Palo Alto Sq.
Palo Alto, CA 94306

Drexel Burnham Lambert, Inc.
5 Palo Alto Sq.
Palo Alto, CA 94306

DSV Partners III
221 Nassau Street
Princeton, NJ 08542

Eastech Associates
One Liberty Sq.
Boston, MA 02109

Fairfield Vent. Mgmt. Co., Inc.
1275 Summer St.
Stamford, CT 06905

New Enterprise Associates, L.P.
235 Montgomery St.
San Francisco, CA 94104

North American Company
111 East Las Olas Blvd.
Fort Lauderdale, FL 33302

Northwest Growth Fund, Inc.
801 Nicollet Mall, Suite 1730
Minneapolis, MN 55402

Oak Management Corp.
2 Railroad Place
Westport, CT 96880

Orange Nassau Capital Corp.
260 Franklyn St.
Boston, MA 02110

Pioneer Ventures Company
113 East 55th Street
New York, NY 10022

Idanta Partners
201 Main St
Fort Worth, TX 76102

Scientific Advances, Inc.
601 W 5th Ave
Columbus, OH 43201

Security Pacific Capital Corp.
5 Palo Alto Sq.
Palo Alto, CA 94304

Sprout Capital Groups
140 Broadway
New York, NY 10005

Stephenson Merchant Banking
100 Garfield
Denver, CO 80206

Sutter Hill Ventures
Two Palo Alto Sq.
Palo Alto, CA 94306

T.A. Associates
445 Milk St.
Boston, MA 02109

Morgenthaler Mngt. Co.
200 National City Bank Bldg.
Cleveland, OH 44114

Narragansett Capital Corp.
40 Westmenster St.
Providence, RI 029093

NBR II
P.O. Box 796
Addison, TX 75001

New England Enterprise Capital
One Washington Mall
Boston, MA 02108

Venrock Associates
2 Palo Alto Sq.
Palo Alto, CA 94306

Vista Corporation
701 B St.
San Diego, CA 92101

The Wallner Company
215 Coast Blvd.
La Jolla, CA 92037

Warburg, Pincus Capital Corp.
466 Lexington Ave
New York, NY 10017

Welsh, Carson, Anderson & Stowe
One World Financial Center
New York, NY 10281

Whitehead Associates, Inc.
15 Valley Drive
Greenwich, CT 06830

Regional Financial Enterprises
36 Grove St.
New Canaan, CT 06840

SAS Associates
515 So. Figueroa St.
Los Angeles, CA 90071

Technology Venture Investors
3000 Sand Hill Rd.
Menlo Park, CA 94025

The Hillman Co.
2000 Grant Building
Pittsburg, PA 15219

Venture Cap. Fund of New England
160 Federal St
Boston, MA 02110

Union Venture Corporation
445 So. Figueroa St.
Los Angeles, CA 90071

Woodland Capital Company
3007 Skyway Circle N.
Irving, TX 75038

Xerox Corporation
2029 Century Park E.
Los Angeles, CA 90067.

Section Two

How To Run A Business And Collect Income At Home

Cash Through The Mail

How To Make Money As A Commission Circular Mailer

There are many mail-order publications that will list your name in this directory "COMMISSION CIRCULARS WANTED." List your name under this classification and dealers will mail bundles of circulars to you with a blank space at the bottom of the ad in which you stamp your name. You mail these out and the ads "appear" to be your own. You receive money for whatever is advertised on the circular, you keep 50%, and the dealer who sent you the circulars will fill the orders for the other half. The idea is...NEVER ever mail out a single circular by itself. Mail as many as you can of the different circulars. Stuff your envelopes FULL. The more you mail out to one customer, the more likely you are to make a sale. Make no mistake about it, they do read these circulars. Next, run ads in different magazines saying you mail circulars for others.

Charge whatever you feel is fair, but the standard rate is $20 per thousand 8½ x 11" circulars mailed. Always, in your ads, mention that "We mail commission circulars FREE." Whichever part of the ad the reader responds to, you make money. It is possible to run this business into a full-time job and make $15,000 to $20,000 a year. The best plan is to follow up and keep growing. Take on new commission circulars, test them, keep the ones that pull, omit the ones that don't pull. Before you know it, you'll graduate from a part-time to a full-time mailer.

How To Mail 1,000 Big Mails Free

Keep advertising. Place at least one ad a day until you are receiving an average of 34 a day or 1,000 a month. If you use the following ad, this plan will not be hard to implement: "How to mail out 1000 big mails. FREE! Complete plan, 25 cents (your name & address)." The 25-cents plan weighs only 1/10 of an ounce or less and will go 3rd class for the minimum postage. You can fill the envelope with another 1 and 9/10 oz. (9½ sheets size 8½ x 11, or 70 size 3 x 6) for a free ride without paying additional postage. In other words, you make up a big mail weighing 1 & 9/10 oz. or less and you can mail it out for free with the plans you advertise. This "Big Mail" can include imprints that pay you a commission or you can charge others for mailing their circulars inside your envelopes. The main point is that ads selling the 25-cents plans will pull many more orders than just "Big Mail 25 Cents." A good dealer will take in about $100 a month with ads like these.

Ten Steps That Put You In The Commission Mailing Business

1) Order a rubber stamp with your name and address on it. **2)** Send for free imprints (commission circulars); you pay only the postage for these. **3)** Send for some free names who want a big mail. **4)** Buy 100 envelopes and 100 stamps. **5)** Address the envelopes to the name wanting big mail. **6)** When you receive your circulars, stamp your name and address in the blank space on the commission side of the imprint. **7)** Put one circular in each envelope. **8)** Mail them. **9)** When you receive orders, take out your commission. **10)** Forward everything else to the source (the individual or firm) that sent you the circulars. YOU ARE NOW IN BUSINESS. If you are serious about commission mailing, you have to take time to look over each offer you receive. All you need to do is follow the 10 steps above. Be happy with $60 to $150 a week made in your spare time (from 2 to 4 hours each night and no less than 5 night a week). Then, you too, can make money mailing. There is money in mailing—I know, because I do it. But believe me, it is not as some would advertise it. You will not get rich overnight. You won't make $50,000 and work only one hour each week. NO! You will be able to invest and grow as big as you wish, but always remember to stuff each envelope FULL!

How To Get 6,000 Circulars Printed And Mailed For Free

Here is a plan that will enable you to get your circulars printed and mailed FREE, plus reduce the cost of your own mailing to nothing. Locate an offset printer in your area or by mail order in one of the many mail order publications who will print both sides of an 8½ x 11 for $14 per 1000. Then run the following ad over your name in any mail order publication. A letterpress publication needs no camera-ready copy. Ad copy: co-op printing (our ad on back side) 1,000 2½ x 5½ only $3.25. Send one camera-ready copy to: (your name and address) or: Circulars Printed (our ad on back side) 1,000 3x6 only $3.25 (your name and address). On an 8½ x 11 sheet of paper, you get six 3x6 circulars from responses to your ad, plus six 3x6's on the other side FREE. Have the printer cut them into six 3x6's 1,000 each. Send 1,000 to each of your customers. You get 6,000 of your side printed FREE, and mailed by your customers FREE. Six responses to your ad will give you $19.50-$15.50 to print and cut the 3x6's and $4 for mailing the circulars back to your customers. If printing and postage costs go up, as they do again and again, adjust your price accordingly. Check the mail-order publications to see what others charge for printing.

How To Make $50 Mailing 150 Envelopes

Order 5,000 3 x 6 commission circulars from your printer selling $1 items and paying you 50% commission on every order you receive. Have your name printed on them—it will save hours of stamping time. Then mail 100 each to 50 "Exchange Mailers" in 50 envelopes—mark them X-10-SY which means "Exchange 100 send yours." When you receive 100 circulars from each 150 envelopes mail your 5000 circulars. If you have a good circular offering a popular seller and the exchange mailers you sent yours to are honest and dependable, you should receive 2% returns. This will bring you $50 profit. That is the complete plan, and it works. It is working every day for many mailers.

The $50 Per Thousand Advertising Plan

This is a woman's true story about addressing envelopes at home in her spare time for $50 per thousand. Mrs. R., realizing that straight addressing only produces $8 to $15 per 1000, decided to work out the following original plan. While searching for some new idea, she noticed that local firms were tying in some of their special offers with birthdays and marriages (in other words, they were mailing their offer to customers or prospects in these two fields). This plan intrigued Mrs. R. and she interviewed one store manager about the subject and learned that an elaborate filing system was necessary in order to mail their special offers to folks having birthdays, or just married or having anniversaries, to say nothing of blessed events. She also learned that this particular store was quite willing to shift the filing and mailing burden onto someone else's shoulder. So here was a ready-made service for Mrs. R. She offered a service to this and other stores, agreeing to furnish the names of such people, keeping file cards on each name collected, and stuff the firm's envelopes with their circulars, then mail them out. She set a modest price of 5 cents per name and the store furnished all circulars, envelope, and stamps for each mailing. Since these mailings were costing 12 to 16 cents per mail package, her services and fees seemed most attractive. By specializing in this one field, she could do it at a lower price than the stores could do it themselves. Other stores were eager to take advantage of this service and she soon had a growing business.

Earn $100 A Week In A Business Everyone Can Operate

Here is a business anyone can operate making excellent profits. This is NOT a little-known business and you are probably aware of it. The business I am writing about is NAME LISTS. One New York firm boasts profits of over $100,000 a year selling names to direct mail houses. YOU CAN DO IT TOO. I don't guarantee you will make $100,000 a year selling names but you can easily make $100 each and every week if you follow these simple instructions. **1)** Run the following advertisement over your name: "Receive hundreds of BIG MAILS FREE. Get listed for 10 cents." When names begin coming in, type them on name and address labels which you get at stationery stores. **2)** Sell your lists for about $1.50 per 100 names and $20 per thousand (many charge $40 per thousand). **3)** Make a list of the major mail-order houses which advertise in the mechanics and women's magazines and send a printed post card to each of them explaining your offer to sell mail-order names to them typed on gummed labels. **4)** The original remittance of 10 cents you receive from the individuals who requested to be listed with you will pay for your acknowledgments to them (and you can enclose your other offers to these people for profits).

Riches From Your Rubber Stamp

A good income can be a reality for anyone owning a rubber stamp. The only additional items needed are envelopes, postage stamps, and a few commission circulars. The rubber stamp is the only one of the above items you will need to pay for. The envelopes, postage stamps and circulars can be obtained for FREE. Many small operators are earning a comfortable living as commission mailers. The tricks of the trade are rather involved, but I'll give you all the basic information you'll need to start a profitable business. Hundreds of supply houses are constantly looking for people to mail their circulars—for FREE. However, they need to know that you are in business or they cannot send circulars to you. Start your commission mailing business by running this short classified ad in as many ad sheets and magazines as your investment will allow: "Commission circulars mailed free. Must pay me 50% or more. Send postage paid; (your name and address)." The above ad will bring plenty of free imprint circulars to you. As they come in, insert one of the circulars from each batch into a notebook and list the source of the items and the address to avoid confusion when filling any future orders. While waiting for your first package of circulars to arrive, place the following small ad in as many ad sheets as you can afford, offering a big mail for free: "Free Big Mail! Return this ad with self-addressed, stamped envelope (your name and address)." The above ad will bring free stamps and envelopes to you. The people who answer this type of ad are interested in seeing what you have to offer and are usually excellent prospects. In the beginning you will probably mail no more than 100 envelopes per month. As your income grows, you can expand your monthly mailings. Some commission mailers mail thousands of pieces per month.

How To Co-Publish For Maximum Profits

There are many fine trade magazines and ad sheets that you may co-publish in the mail-order business. Some of the better ones are Mail Sale Advertiser, Mail-Order Bulletin, Popular Advertiser, The Enterpriser and Easy Chair Shopper. They reach an amazing number of small homeworkers and opportunity seekers. If your product or service appeals to these readers, the rates are right. The prime reasons for using these magazines are: **1)** We get a 50% discount on our advertising after the first time in exchange for mailing a few copies. **2)** We earn 50% commission on all new co-publishers and advertisers that we get for the publishers. Of course we hope to do some business from our own advertising also. How does the system work? After you place your advertisement at the first time rate, you will receive a discount on all future advertising as long as you continue to co-publish that magazine. That discount on your ads and a commission on the others is usually 50%. In return for the discount you are expected to mail a few copies—honestly. Include the copies in orders with big mails or advertise them free for the postage. Using these methods, your postage cost to mail your copies is zero. Another reason for co-publishing various magazines is that many of them do not require camera-ready copy. Some do an excellent job of typesetting and it's free to you. Items selling in these publications usually sell for $3 or less with $1 being a heavy seller. Remember, it doesn't cost you to advertise—it PAYS.

How To Make Money With Your Own Ad Sheets

Usually ad sheets are started by the publisher cutting ads from other magazines and making his paste-ups with these "freebies". The beginner then mails his ad sheet to these dealers and asks them to rerun their ads with his at "X" number of dollars per column-inch. This is a risky beginning because many dealers will not buy additional ad space for one reason or another, but it is worth a try.

How To Double Your Earnings In Mail-Order

Want to double your earnings in mail-order? You can if you use my simple method! I've used it for years and still do. Begin by running one or two ads in several different mail-order publications. When orders begin coming in, take a full 50% of the profits and invest them in more advertising. Most dealers don't do this and wonder why they aren't making money. You must invest at least ½ your profits to DOUBLE your income in this business. In addition to investing profits, multiplying the number of products or services can be of additional help in expanding your business. When I started in mail-order, I had $5 to invest. I didn't believe it would be enough to help but it was, and I showed a profit of over $300 in my first 3 months. That wasn't a bad beginning, but today I bring in many times my original investment each day. Investment of profits is the secret if you wish to succeed in business and mail-order is no exception.

Cash From Telephone Services

Dial A Fortune

One profitable telephone business in the 976 pay-per call information industry. This relatively new business is experiencing explosive growth because it gives entrepreneurs a chance to go into business with the phone company and provide the public with valuable and/or entertaining information. It's not unusual to hear of many information providers bringing in gross sales of $10,000 to $30,000 per month, paid to them by the phone company in one monthly check.

The most successful phone lines are the computerized, high tech lines. For example, 976-WAVE will give you the surf conditions for a number of beaches. A computer will ask you which beach you are interested in and will instruct which button to press in order to hear the report for that area. The computer will then switch you to the right message for that beach.

Almost every kind of information can be obtained from a 976 line such as sports score updates, humor lines, stock exchange reports, soap opera updates, horoscopes, and countless other program ideas. The service operation is fairly simple: the 976 line owners determine the price which his callers will pay (which is usually about $2.00) and the phone company adds the charge onto the caller's phone bill. Any additional toll charges are also added. The phone company then remits a percentage of the charge to the information provider. For example, Pacific Bell will remit approximately $1.60 of a $2.00 charge to the information provider and retain the remainder as their profit.

Because 976 equipment is extremely expensive to purchase, many newcomers to the business rent their equipment and the shelf space to hold it. The offices are set up close to the phone company as most of them require that 976 equipment be stationed within close proximity to their central office. The machine rental fees range from $400 to $900 per month. After the installation charge and the equipment rental fees have been paid for the first few months, the initial **hard costs** of starting a 976 line can be kept under $4,000 to $5,000. The information provider should always take the variable expenses for programing and advertising into account. Also, the information access business means that you are selling information which should be considered valuable. Therefore, you must make sure your service is marketable and will be purchased by many.

Earn Money Selling Magazines By Telephone

You can also sell periodicals direct or by mail. The magazine agencies listed below will send you all the information you need to get started in selling magazine subscriptions. Write to them for information if you are interested.

McGregor Magazine Agency, Subscription Services, Inc., Mount Morris, IL 61054

Franklin Square Subscription Agency, 545 Cedar Ln., Teaneck, NJ 07666

Crowley, 305 E. 204th St., Bronx, NY 10467

Use Your Phone To Be A Telemarketer

A great way to work from your home is to make your services available to match housing and remodeling contractors with customers who need to have work done on their homes. To do this, you will need to establish a list of homeowners by contacting them and offering them a place in a homeowners' association which you have established. When one of them needs a remodeling or housing contractor, all they need to do is to call you. You will contact a specially screened contractor to complete their work for them. What homeowner could refuse this easy and convenient system?

In time, you may find that the volume of business is more than you can handle and you will have to hire a number of employees. Then you can sit at home and collect money from the calls they receive. Some people have made as much as **$20,000 a week by simply answering their phone** using this system. There is an exciting book concerning this telephone money system called **$100,000 Phone Calls** which is available at Lion Publishing Co., 6150 Mission Gorge Rd., Suite 225, San Diego, CA, 92120, for just $10.00.

Cash From Magazine And Newspaper Advertisements

287 Profit-Making Ads

If you haven't read about this ad before, you will be excited to read it now: "287 Profit-Making Ads—Sell under your name. Earn 50-100% on drop-shipments. Earning potential $370. Seven sheets, 189 ads paying 50% ; 67 paying 75%; 28 all-profit ads, dealership set-up $2. Moore's Enterprise, 2639 Merhoff St., Louisville, KY 40217". We sent off for the above offer and found that Joseph Moore, the owner, had expanded and improved the dealership set-up since January. He added more and better deals: All items selling less than $1 or more that pay 75% commission—all drop-ship. What's more, Joe has one single price: $15 Special for all he's got. Hundreds of offers and reports in a BIG envelope including the right to reprint and sell these items for 100% profit.

How To Earn $1,000 To $100,000 Reading Newspapers

Act as a "Finder"—a person who gets a cash fee from the seller, and buyer. Example: Suppose you read in the newspaper or hear about a person who has a million-dollar building to sell, and you just happen to know of another person who might be interested in this kind of real estate. You then merely contact the seller, tell him you have a potential buyer whom you will introduce to him if the seller will pay you a 2% commission fee. If he agrees, you introduce the prospective buyer to him. Then, if the buyer and seller get together on a deal, you will EARN a $20,000 commission (2% of the selling price). The introduction can be made in person or by mail. And it is possible for you to find hundreds of these opportunities by checking the classified section of the major business and local papers.

How To Publish A Contest Bulletin

Many people are now entering various contests to reap the benefits that their jobs cannot provide them. These hopefuls rationalize that "one day I will win." You can help these individuals discover a whole new world by providing Contest Bulletins. One man in Florida publishes a monthly bulletin and accumulates many friends and a large profit through his service. Using an inexpensive mimeograph machine, he lists various contests, rules and addresses where entries are to be sent. He gets his information by reading the latest issues of many national magazines. His customers are obtained from ads in local and national media. At fifty cents per copy, it can be said that his business is not only profitable but successful as well. His present circulation is now in the thousands.

Savings And Investments

How To Get 300% More Interest From Your Savings Account

If two banks pay interest semi-annually, do both banks pay the same interest? No. The amount of interest banks pay depends on their book-keeping practices. A subtle difference in these practices can mean a 300% earnings difference! Here's why: One bank could pay 5¼% interest from the day of deposit on the minimum balance held in the account over a six-month period. Another bank may pay 5¼% interest from the average balance in the account over the same period.

Get Up To One Million Dollars Life Insurance With No Cash

Contact: Bridge Capital Corp., 140 Mineola Blvd., Mineola, NY 11501. This firm claims they can place life insurance policies with nationally recognized companies. You pay NO cash but exchange your surplus inventory or services or unregistered stock, furniture, lots of different products, and other items, services, etc.

How To Get 52% On Your Savings

If you invest your money in foreign banks, such as banks in Mexico, you can pull in an incredible return on your money. Some institutions pay as much as 52% interest on a savings account. In return for this high rate of return, you must take the chance that the bank will not fail and the currency of the country is not devalued in some way. You may also run into problems taking your money out of this country. For more details, contact Mexletter, Hamburgo 165, Mexico D.F.C.

More Than $300,000 by Age 55!

Yes, it's possible to reach this goal. Through a regular and simple savings plan that most people can handle without financial hardship, deposit $2000 each year in one of the higher yielding savings plans and keep it there. Suppose you start this plan when you are 25 years old. While future interest rates are impossible to predict, we will figure at a 10% accrued yield. At this yield, by the age of 55 you would have accumulated a nest egg of over $300,000! This principal will draw over $30,000 per year and more in later years if you continue the plan. Start a systematic and determined savings plan while you are young. You can enjoy the benefits of wealth at the still-youthful age of 55!

Own Your Own Million-Dollar Corporation In 4 Weeks

It is possible to appear to be a millionaire in four weeks and it is very easy to do. Another thing I have learned is that it is possible to create this illusion of wealth—and to use this illusion to become wealthy. All this is possible because in today's computerized, impersonal world, it only takes the appearance of wealth to make money.

People believe what they see. If you appear wealthy and successful, to them you are. It's only human nature to judge a book by its cover. And by merely appearing wealthy, you can perhaps even become wealthy because success attracts money and power.

The plan to appear to be worth $1,000,000 in four weeks is very simple and easy. First, form a corporation in the state of Delaware. For more information on forming a corporation write: Corporation Services Co., 1013 Center Rd., Wilmington, DE. The big thing is that no proof of capitalization is required in Delaware. You can therefore issue yourself one thousand shares of stock in the corporation and assign a value of $1,000 to each share. This gives your corporation a paper value of one million dollars. You do not have to live in Delaware to form a corporation there.

How To Add $100,000 To A Business Balance Sheet—For $50

You can add $100,000 or more to your balance sheet if you already own a business. Set up a corporation in Delaware and add the corporate stock as assets to your balance sheet.

Own a Business With No Cash Investment

This could be your first step to riches. Look for a business whose owner, for various reasons, desperately wants out but is unable to find a buyer. Perhaps due to disinterest or poor management it isn't making a profit. Offer to pay the book value from a certain percentage of profits. The owner might consider this proposal rather than chance the business failing completely. Have a lawyer draw up the transfer of ownership and the other conditions of the agreement. Most should be to your advantage.

You must, of course, consider only a business with the potential of earning good profits through your ability and efforts. A financing source should be ready to help if you need funds for expansion.

Establishing And Using Credit To Your Advantage

Wipe Out Debts Without Bankruptcy

In 1938, a federal law was passed known as the Wage Earner Plan. It is administrated by the same branch of our courts that handles bankruptcy. You must be a wage-earner to use the law—that is the primary requirement. The Wage Earner plan does not, in itself, ''wipe out'' debts, but a little known proviso of your filing requires that your creditors appear. Statistics indicate that 40% fail to appear, in which case those debts are indeed ''wiped out''. In some cases, 100% of the creditors fail to appear, which enables you to wipe out ALL your debts without bankruptcy. If some of the creditors do appear, then the court allows you to spread your payments out over a three-year period in smaller amounts that you can afford to pay. Once you file, you stop bill collectors, lawsuits, judgments, assignments, seized bank accounts, and other actions against you. And to top it off, your credit rating is, in many cases, improved because you made an honest effort to work with the lending firms. Additionally, if the seller used deceptive trade practices to induce your purchase, your debt may be wiped out under the provisions of the Uniform Commercial Code. Under the Homestead Act, your residence can be exempted from any levy to the extent determined by local law. Check with your local courthouse.

This is only one of the great tips included in the book **"Erase Bad Debt"** from Lion Publishing. You can buy this helpful book for just $15.00 by writing to them at 6150 Mission Gorge Rd, #225, San Diego, CA, 92120.

How To Raise Up To $50,000 With Your Credit Cards

In today's ''credit world'', virtually everyone has credit cards. Millions of Americans carry these cards; some people have as many as thirty. Credit limits on these cards average about $1,000 per card. With just your credit cards, you can get over $15,000 in cash and merchandise.

Even hard-to-get credit cards like American Express and Carte Blanc will be easy to get once you have cards like Master Card and Visa. Credit limits on American Express and Carte Blanc are as high as $20,000. Combining these cards with cards like Visa and Master Charge can give you credit up to $50,000 for 60 days with no interest.

You can also use department store cards to gather quick cash! Simply go to the stores which issued you a card and charge some merchandise. A few days later, return the merchandise for a merchandise credit slip instead of crediting your account. This slip can be used for future purchases and is as good as cash in that particular store. Now you can sell these credit slips to your friends and neighbors for a 10% discount. Since this money is to be used for an investment, you should make sure the investment will pay higher than 10%. Again, if you began this plan right after your monthly billing notice, you will have use of the money for 60 days at no interest from the department store.

This type of creative financing is explained in detail in the book **"Become A Millionaire From Credit Cards Even If You Have Bad Credit."** I highly recommend this publication, which is available from Lion Publishing Co., at 6150 Mission Gorge Rd., #225, San Diego, CA, 92120, for just $15.00.

How To Borrow Money Interest-Free

There are a number of ways to borrow money interest-free if you take the time to operate the methods. However, one of the simplest ways is to borrow it from a bank which offers "overdraft protection." You've seen these offers by banks which extend to you a loan for the amount you overdraw your checking account. By setting up two or more (and the credit limits can go up to $5,000 each) you can write yourself a "loan" from one bank, cover the loan with a deposit from another bank where you have overdraft checking and then repeat the process every day or two. By covering each withdrawal with another deposit, you will not be charged interest since it would take two or three days for the records to catch up—by that time you've made another deposit which covered the original loan. Operated like that, you can keep the money interest-free for quite some time.

Establish "AAA" Credit In 30 Days

To work this plan you need at least $400 to begin. You should borrow this from your friends if necessary. Then go to a bank of your choice and deposit the $400 into a regular passbook savings account. Wait a few days for the account to be posted and return to the bank to ask for a $400 loan, offering the passbook as collateral. Since the bank's already holding your $400, there is no way it can loose by lending you another $400 and they won't even make a credit check. Then, with your borrowed $400, you go to another bank, open a savings account, return a few days later, and borrow $400 from that bank all the time using your passbook as collateral. Then repeat the process at a third bank with your borrowed $400. Wait a few days and go to a fourth bank where you open a CHECKING account. Wait a few days and make a payment on each of the other three loans. A week later, make payments again on the three loans, and continue paying each week until you have paid off the balance. A credit investigation at this point will show you with three active bank loans (which are considered hard to get), a checking account, and a paying history for the three bank loans—with you having paid up in advance. Thus, you have AAA credit in as little as 30 days. From here you go on to apply for loans, credit cards, and other items on credit. For a more detailed look at this subject, get ahold of the book **"How To Raise Millions With Credit Cards Regardless If You Are In Debt."** This book is offered for $15.00 through Lion Publishing Co. at 6150 Mission Gorge Rd. #225, San Diego, CA 92120.

How To Raise Tremendous Amounts Of Capital —Up To $50,000,000

This method of raising capital consists of placing a classified ad in the business opportunities section of your Sunday newspaper. Here are a few examples:

Will pay XX% (insert percentage) interest on small loan for a short period. Sound collateral. Your name and phone number.

Advertise in the "Business Opportunities" or "Capital Wanted" section of the paper. You can raise millions using this method.

How To Raise $200,000 In 24 Hours

Many people have had opportunities presented to them where quick cash was necessary. Literally dozens, maybe hundreds, of these super bargains are available every day in your city or town. Most people are unable to take advantage of these great opportunities because of a lack of cash. A simple process is available where you will be able to generate quick cash within 24 hours.

The process is easy and quick and can be completed in about 1 year. After working this plan, you will be able to generate up to $200,000 in 24 hours. You will be able to take advantage of all super bargains that come your way. Believe me, the power to raise this kind of cash in such a short time will surely let you turn the corner on your road to riches.

You can call this plan the banking round robin. Go to ten banks and tell the loan officer at each that you want to borrow $1,000 for 30 days. Upon paying off your loans, wait 30 days and go back to each bank from which you borrowed the initial $1,000. This time, request a larger amount depending on what you think your bank will loan, like $5,000. If each bank approves a $5,000 loan, you will be able to raise $50,000 in this second step.

Continue this step-by-step process. Each time you go to the bank, ask for a larger amount and a longer pay-back period. What you are doing, of course, is establishing a millionaire's credit reputation by repetition. That is, you always pay back the money when it is due, and by being prompt, combined with the number of loans you've made and paid, you will have established a very powerful credit rating and relationship with the institutions.

After about a year of using this process, you should be able to borrow $20,000 from each bank on your signature. Using 10 banks in this plan, you will be able to borrow up to $200,000 on your signature in as little as 24 hours.

How To Borrow Huge Amounts Of Cash

Here's how to borrow up to $50 million. The first step is to organize a ''syndicate'' or real estate ''trust.'' Your attorney can help you set these up depending on what you need the money for. Either of these legal entities can sell ''stock'' or ''shares'' to the public if your proposed investment is worthwhile. By utilizing the services of a stockbroker and competent accountants, attorneys, etc., it is possible to attract HUGE amounts of capital for any business proposition you stand to benefit from.

Get Any Credit Card You Want

You should have no problem getting any credit card you want if you follow the above procedure first. However, there are a few rules to follow to ensure you have no difficulties in obtaining your cards. **1)** Apply for department store cards first. Purchase something and pay balance when due. **2)** Apply for gasoline credit cards listing your department store cards as references. **3)** Apply for bank cards—Master Charge & Visa. **4)** Apply for the Travel & Entertainment cards—American Express, Diner's Club, etc.

How To Take Over A Going Business With Zero Cash

Here is another little-known technique which can help make you wealthy virtually overnight. The reason is because when you take over a business, you also take over the salary of the owner—and that can often be as much as $75,000 yearly.

To get started, you should look for a business that is in deep trouble—one that is about to go bankrupt. Many of these businesses can be acquired with little or no down payment. They could be manufacturing, service businesses, real estate based businesses, or almost any other type. Why should someone offer a business for zero cash down? Here's why:

- The owner of a failing business will be glad to get out from under his bills and headaches.
- He believes the business is beyond saving.
- Finding a buyer for a heavily indebted business is extremely difficult.

There are plenty of these cash-free takeovers available and often advertised. What you have to do is look for them. Search through business ads in newspaper classifieds and trade magazines, check with local business brokers and local real estate agents who also handle business sales.

Find out everything—Once you have found a suitable business, you must get all the details concerning it. For instance, you will have to find out how much the business owes and to whom, as well as the value of the building and property itself.

What you are looking for are the firms whose inventory and assets are higher than their debts. You must also consider the sales income and expenses in operating the business. Look for such things as the gross sales, selling and labor costs, taxes, and so on. This information can come from the firm's account books, income tax returns, or from an accountant's certified statement.

Make an offer—Explain your belief to the owner that you think you can turn the business around and make it profitable, but it will take at least two years. Since this is your plan, here is a typical offer you make to the owner:

Zero Cash Down
Offer Him Promissory Notes
No Note Payments For Two Years
Offer To Pay All The Debts Of The Company

Now be sure to have your lawyer draw up a proper sales agreement before buying. You should also try for an arrangement to pay the attorney's legal fees from business funds—not from your own pocket.

If you find that you absolutely must give the owner a nominal down payment, you can use any of the capital-raising methods described earlier. However, you must insist on paying the bulk of the price with promissory notes. And you should insist that payments do not begin for a year—preferably two. You will need that long to turn the business around and show a profit.

Once you have acquired your sick business, you must take steps to make it profitable. The first step is to deal with the creditors. Here is what you do:

Set up an appointment with each creditor to discuss the firm's indebtedness. Explain to them that you have just taken over the business and you would like to pay off all the debts as soon as possible. Tell them the business has no cash at the moment but that you hope to start showing a profit in six months to a year. Your strategy is to convince the creditor to accept a reduced settlement of the debt.

First, try to get a debt reduction of from 30 to 70 percent from the total debt. You must also insist that no payments begin for at least one year. Your third request will be for a long term repayment plan—10 years, if possible.

Once your creditor has accepted the offer, make it legal by getting him to sign an agreement. Through this maneuver alone, your business will have reduced its debt by 30 to 70 percent, lowered payment, recovered from its sickness, but you don't stop here. You can also:

1. Sell off excess inventories: Finished goods or raw materials.
2. Sell off part of your production machinery.
3. Sell more stock in your firm.
4. Sell off a division or separate department.
5. Split your company into separate firms and sell the stock.
6. Make any other cost cuts you can: Reduce payroll, find cheaper supply sources, eliminate waste, etc.
7. Eliminate products, services, or accounts which are marginally profitable.

8. Study how to increase sales and locate new markets.

Incredible as it may sound, there are many businesses that can be saved through these methods. All too frequently, owners are completely unaware of the true value of their business. In many cases, the owner has exhausted his operating capital and credit through mismanagement. Your offer allows him to recoup some of his investment, and your offer may be the only one he gets!

The Corporate Takeover—You can use a variation of the promissory note method by offering the owner corporate stock as a down payment, or even as full payment if the owner is really desperate. Assuming you set up a corporation with 10 other investors, the owner would be assured of a sales potential of 10 customers for his stock once the business gets going.

Tax Tips For Investors And Entrepreneurs

1) Set up a corporation: The tax rate on the first $25,000 of retained profits is low. You can set up a medical expense reimbursement plan for yourself without including any employees. Your corporation can own and claim depreciation deductions on your car. Even if you are in business part time, you can set up a tax sheltered retirement savings plan.

2) Work a swap if products or services at every opportunity. Both you and the other guy will save a lot in taxes. Neither of you will have as much recorded profit on a swap transaction. Hence, you pay less tax.

3) Avoid employees: Have your work done by self-employed independent contractors and save on Social Security Taxes, Unemployment Taxes and Workman's Compensation Insurance.

4) If you carry an inventory, use the L.I.F.O. (Last-in first-out) method of valuing your inventory. Your non-deductible inventory will consist of the oldest items bought before price increases, and you will be deducting the highest-priced materials or merchandise.

5) If you are trying to sell stock or are going to invest in a small corporation, ask your Tax Advisor about the special section 1224 election. If the Corporation goes under, the investor can deduct up to $50,000 against ordinary income and, if it succeeds, he gets capital gains when he sells out.

6) To nail down a capital gain, you must hold the property for more than six months. One extra day over six months can make a big difference.

7) Check with the local Federal Unemployment Office about hiring workers under the W.I.N. Program. You can get a tax credit of up to 20% of a qualifying employee's first year's wages. It's a real steal.

8) You can accumulate up to $100,000 in profits (after paying a 22% tax on the first $25,000 per year) in a corporation and pay a tax on only half of the accumulated amount (by capital gains route) if you liquidate instead of paying yourself a salary or dividends. This is a very attractive pitch for investors in short-term (5-10 year) ventures.

9) When in doubt, deduct. The probability of an audit for small businesses with less than $30,000 income is very low. Chances are, your deduction will go through and even if it doesn't, it will only cost you the tax you would have paid plus 6% of that tax. Just be sure you have a valid reason for your deduction. But, don't get caught on a fraud charge. It isn't worth it.

Recommended reading: "The April Game" by Diolenes ($7.95), published by the Playboy Press, and distributed by Simon and Schuster, Inc., N.Y. (1973).

NOTE: The preceding items are offered for general information only, and the reader is cautioned to seek competent tax counsel before using any of the above comments or information.

How To Raise Up To $50,000 With Your Credit Cards

Millions of people have an assortment of credit cards in today's almost cashless society. With many bank credit cards, and even department store cards, it is possible to apply under the "same name" and obtain two or more identical cards bearing only different account numbers. Given the high limits on cards such as American Express ($20,000) and others, it is a simple procedure to raise up to $50,000 by utilizing 30 to 40 cards or less if you use American Express. With the bank cards, you simply obtain a "cash advance" up to your credit limit. With American Express and Carte Blanc cards, you can charge merchandise such as gold coins and turn around and sell it at a discount to your friends, neighbors, etc. With enough cards, you can quickly turn any amount of discounted "merchandise" into cash. A fine book which details this process is Carl Simon's **"How To Raise Millions With Credit Cards—Regardless If You Are In Debt."** You can get this book through Lion Publishing Co., 6150 Mission Gorge Rd., #225, San Diego, CA, 92120. The price is just $15.00.

Unique Businesses

How To Get Rich Without Working

"Working" is described as the obligation to attend regularly and perform a designated task. An obligation that usually consumes eight or nine hours of one's daily life. "The Rat Race", it is humorously called, yet most people must depend on such jobs to finance their basic necessities of life.

How have some people become wealthy without restricting themselves to "work?" Some have been lucky enough to inherit a fortune. Others have struck it rich in lotteries or by gambling. A successful business owner, an officer in a large corporation, or a super salesman might acquire wealth through aggressive personal characteristics.

Then there are those who, through manipulation, inside knowledge or proper timing, have acquired a windfall by investing in the stock or commodity market.

Talented people have become rich as inventors, authors, sports figures, TV and movie stars. Professional people such as lawyers, doctors and bankers, through high fees or salaries, become wealthy.

The above situations, matters of luck, special talent or timing, are beyond the hope of the average working man or woman. Yet, there are many opportunities for anyone to make a lot of money without relying on luck, high education or special abilities. First of all, those who have acquired wealth through their own personal efforts outline this advice for necessary attitudes and desires to acquire a high financial standing:

1. Go where the money is—get your share.
2. Be willing to accept and take business risks.
3. Do something positive in your search for riches.
4. Be willing to start small and grow big.
5. Be ready to jump into million-dollar markets if the opportunity presents itself.
6. Use other people's money to help build your own wealth.
7. Diversify to increase your income.
8. Create, locate and market something unique and different.

Long ago, someone with a wise observation noted, "Working won't make your rich." So, let's review some of the methods others have used to become wealthy, and ways which you too, can acquire riches that a salaried job will never provide.

Becoming a "Finder"

This is perhaps the easiest way to earn big money. What is a "Finder?" A finder is a person who brings two parties together on a transaction and collects a fee for arranging the meeting that consummated the deal. The fee may be a percentage of the transaction for a flat determined sum.

Let's explain your role as a finder. Suppose you learn of someone who is interested in selling a large parcel of land, a building, surplus merchandise, a business, or dozens of other high-priced items. You contact this person or firm and advise that you can furnish the name of a prospective buyer for a finder's fee if the sale is completed. You introduce the prospective buyer to the seller by letter and let those two parties come to an agreement on the deal. You are entitled to a commission for locating the parties and arranging the meeting that resulted in completing the transaction.

Where do you find these opportunities? You may be fortunate enough to find them in your own area. Look and ask around. Note "For Sale" signs on large acreage or buildings. Check "Wanted" and "For Sale" listings in newspaper classified sections, "The Wall Street Journal", "Business Opportunities Journal", or subscribe to some of the publications that advertise offers suitable for a finder.

Never contact the seller, except for particulars of his offer, until you have a definite buyer prospect. After your initial contact with both parties, send all correspondence concerning referrals, names and confirmation of finder's fees by registered mail. Keep a copy of all correspondence in case any legal problem arises concerning the receipt of your full and due commission.

MONEY FINDER. In a similar method to the above, thousands of people are looking for money for business and commercial activities; others are seeking areas in which to invest. You can operate as a money agent, on a commission basis, by bringing together a party who seeks money with someone who is willing to lend it. Again, contracts may be obtained through the methods outlined above. Don't overlook foreign investors. The Arabs, particularly have billions to invest. Seek such leads in publications with foreign circulation.

Make Money Writing Letters

An Ohio woman earns $50 a week writing personal letters. How? She advertises her services in the National Tabloid Newspapers and ladies' magazines. For $3 weekly, or $10 monthly, she promises to write a long letter to shut-ins, prisoners and service people. Families of these individuals explain the likes and dislikes of those she is to write to and she corresponds along the lines suggested by families and friends.

The $4000 Coupon

Companies spend hundreds and thousands of dollars every day for advertising. Local businesses especially look for effective ways to draw customers to their establishments or to let consumers know of their services. Television and newspaper ads are extremely expensive and only marginally effective. If you could offer an advertising service that would bring customers in, these businesses would give their advertising money to you.

A simple method of alerting customers to a local business is by coupons. Many professional companies produce huge national coupon books to be sold across the country, and you can do the same thing in your city. First, go to a number of small local businesses who are in need of effective advertising. Tell them that you are going to put together a book of coupons to be distributed throughout the local area. (Usually an area or neighborhood from four to eight miles in diameter.) Unlike newspaper or magazine coupons, which have only a 2-4% return rate, direct mail coupons can bring up to a 12% rate of redemption. Business managers know this and will be eager to use your coupons to their advantage.

Once you have accumulated enough businesses to fill your coupon book, it is a simple matter to have the book printed and mailed out to the homes in a specified area. When the local businesses see how their sales pick up, they will want to repeat their advertising with you. Some people make as much as $4,000 a day by publishing coupon books.

Certain businesses which lend themselves to coupon advertising are: small restaurants, card shops, gift shops, arts and craft stores, ice cream parlors, car washes, chimney sweeps, and almost any service related businesses.

Many books have been written on the subject of coupon advertising, but one of the most comprehensive is **Giving Away Special Books,** which can be purchased for $12.00 from Lion Publishing Co., 6150 Mission Gorge Rd., Suite 225, San Diego, CA 92120

Where To Get 3 Sure-Fire Moneymakers Free

Sunshine Greeting Cards are sure profit-makers for part-time selling. You'll be so proud of your contribution to the family income and of those little luxuries you wish for. And you can sell them by inviting the neighbors over for a coffee party and show these nice and beautiful Sunshine cards, gift wrappers and novelties. It's a sure way to earn extra money. You can request everything you need, a free catalog, sales kit, on approval from: Club Sales, Sunshine Art Studios, Inc., 45 Warwick St., Springfield, MA 01102. Extra income can be yours without giving up precious time with your family. Sell this popular greeting card line to all your friends, neighbors and relatives. Over 250 new and different fast-selling greetings and novelties will bring you fast profits.

Bringing In Cash By Collecting Names

People love to enter contests of any kind. You often see contest collection boxes in supermarkets, convenience stores, restaurants, and many of the places you frequent. Anybody can cash in on this great way of making money, and you do not even have to run the contest. Often a business will sponsor a promotional contest and give commissions to independent distributors who send them completed contest entries. All you have to do is to set up contest entry boxes in some local businesses, collect the registration forms that people leave in the box, and send the forms in. Many contest companies will pay between eight and fifteen cents for every name you send in. This can amount to hundreds of dollars every month.

An excellent source of information about this type of business is **The Ultimate Method Of Making Cash.** This book is available for $12.00 from Lion Publishing Co. at 6150 Mission Gorge Road, Suite 225, San Diego, CA 92120.

The Modern, Simple $100-Per-Day Plan

This plan is an old-time proven dollar-puller which is just as effective today as when it was first conceived many years ago.

Not only is this plan profitable in itself but it is an ideal method to obtain names for promotion of other offers.

Here's how this simple plan works:

Run ads similar to this suggested copy: "How would you like to receive 100 letters a day, each containing $1.00? Copy of plan and 15 formulas only $1.00. Rush a dollar to (your name and address)." The money saving formulas are:

Eyeglass Cleaner—Mix together 8 oz. ammonia and 32 oz. denatured alcohol. If you wish to sell the product it can be put in ½ oz. bottles and retailed for $1.00.

Mosquito Repellent—Mix oil of citronella in common Vaseline and apply to hands or on collar of shirt or on a cloth or handkerchief which may be tied around the neck.

Liquid Soap—Shave 2 cakes of laundry soap into 2 gallons of boiling water, add one box sal soda (2½ lbs.). Reduce heat but do not remove from fire until sal soda is dissolved. When cool, add one cup of household ammonia. When this solution has cooled you will have about 2½ gallons of good liquid soap.

Liquid Hand Soap—Dissolve any good powdered soap in boiling water. Add one part alcohol to each 4 parts of soap solution. Perfume base or scent may be added if desired when the solution is cooled.

Powdered Hand Soap—Mix 7 oz. of Tri-Sodium phosphate in sifter with 3 oz. of fine powdered pumice.

Insect and Roach Exterminator—Mix the following: 1 oz. cocoa powder, 1 lb. Borax, 6 oz. powdered sugar, 2 oz. sodium fluoride. Mix well and sprinkle around the areas where insects frequent.

Athlete's Foot Remedy—Mix 4 oz. Borax with a gallon of water. Helps get rid of sores on feet as well. This remedy is for use on feet only.

Liquid Termite Killer—Dissolve 2 lbs. of Para dichlorobenzine into 1 gal. of water. Spray or brush on the areas where termites enter.

Windshield Cleaner—Mix together 3 parts Glycerin, 1 part Alcohol and 2 parts Water. Shake well. This formula also prevents steam and frost from forming on the windshield.

Washing Powder—Mix together thoroughly 15 parts Sodium Sesquicarbonate 2 with 5 parts Trisodium Phosphate. To use, add to the wash water like any other washing powder. Gives excellent cleaning results.

Nail Polish Remover—Mix 6 parts Acetone with 4 parts Ethyl Acetate.

Toilet Bowl Cleaner—Use straight Potassium Acid Sulfate. Sprinkle in the bowl, allow to stand for one hour, then clean with a brush.

Weed Killer—Mix thoroughly 1 lb. of Ferrous Sulfate into 3 gals. of water. To use, spray this solution over weeded areas at sundown.

Drain Pipe Cleaner—Use plain Sodium Hydroxide. Material is toxic, so keep away from skin or clothing.

Cockroach Killer—mix together equal parts of Plaster of Paris and Oatmeal. Sprinkle around areas where cockroaches appear.

These formulas can save you a considerable amount of money for these necessary everyday household products. If you plan to sell any chemical formulas commercially, the preparations may be subject to the Federal Food, Drug and Cosmetic Labeling Act. You can obtain detailed information on such regulation by requesting a free copy of "Digest of the Federal Food, Drug and Cosmetic Act" from the Federal Food and Drug Administration, Washington, DC 20402.

Ingredients for these formulas may be obtained from drug stores, hardware stores or chemical supply houses in your area. If the material is not available locally, write to the following suppliers (typewritten letter on business letterhead).

Chemicals: Frey Scientific Co., 905 Hickory Lane, Mansfield, OH 44905.

Robeco Chemicals Inc., 99 Park Ave., New York, NY 10016. Perfume Bases and Flower Oils: Dodge & Olcott, Inc., 76 9th Ave., New York NY 10011.

Detergent & Soap Bases: Crown Chemical, 1888 Nirvana Ave., Chula Vista, CA 92011.

Names and addresses of other suppliers may be located under appropriate headings or classifications in the Thomas Register or McRae's Blue Book, and both may be found in most public libraries.

To put this plan into operation it is necessary to advertise the $1.00 plan. This can be done by placing the suggested ad in the classified sections of publications with inexpensive larger circulations.

It is also possible to place your offer as a notice on bulletin boards in heavy-traffic areas such as supermarkets, public halls, etc.

When orders come in, have a copy of this report reproduced. It will cost just a few pennies per copy to have it printed. Then mail this report to the people who responded to your ad and submitted the dollar payment. Your customers, in turn, will receive their moneys' worth in information value and the opportunity to buy this plan to work for themselves.

Bear in mind, too, that this plan can be adopted for many other types of offers. Instead of formulas you could offer recipes, business information, or thousands of different matters that people want to learn about. Just change the ad copy to fit your particular offer.

The statement ''100 letters a day, each containing $1.00'' is, of course, rather ambiguous. There is no scientific method to assure an exact figure for mail-order sales or profits. It depends on many factors, such as the amount of advertising or promotion you put forth, and the percentage of orders you receive from this effort. One hundred dollars per day is surely possible; it could even be a lot more!

As mentioned before, this plan is about as "sure-fire" as anything devised for sale through the mail. It requires very little investment and is simple and convenient to operate. It is probably the easiest way for an individual to start a mail-order business and gain experience in this field. And, to emphasize an earlier statement, this is an ideal program to obtain prospects or names for other offers.

Seven Steps To Financial Independence

Profit Ideas is launching a unique mail-order promotion. They will let you promote their seven hard-bound money manuals with brochures they supply for you. Many of their manuals are more than 400 pages long, which makes it very easy to sell them by mail for only $15. For complete free dealership information, write: Profit Ideas, 8361 Vickers St., Suite 304 C, San Diego, CA 92111.

Reporting For Thousands

If you have ever wanted to publish informational articles and reports, you may have a desire that can earn you money in your spare time. Many people find a living by authoring informational reports on health, self-help, diet, or sex. You see some of these people on television talking about their books, explaining how their reports have made them rich.

Your reports need not be as long as this. One man in San Diego authored a five page report which sold for five dollars. He sold 500 of them in one weekend, raking in

$2500 for only a minimal initial investment. Every day he receives more orders for this report over the telephone, and all he has to do is seal the envelopes for his pay.

You can write a report about any subject which you find interesting, but there are some topics that sell better than others. Any type of do-it-yourself article has a wide appeal and has the potential to earn thousands. All you need to do is to complete a simple report, then market it in your local newspapers and periodicals. You can also sell these unique packages in national publications if you feel they have nation-wide appeal. Be sure to let people know how they can receive this valuable by phoning or writing to you.

One book on this subject which you may find quite helpful is **"Unique Packages"** by David Bendah. Lion Publishing Co. at 6150 Mission Gorge Rd., #225, San Diego, CA, 92120 will send it to you for $12.00. I highly recommend it.

How To Become A Money Broker Or Mortgage Broker

The difference between a money broker and a mortgage broker is the mortgage broker deals only in assisting the financing of "mortgages." The money broker handles many types of financial transactions, possibly including "mortgage funding." The only way to get started in either business is to go to your library and learn all you can about banking, monetary sciences, accounting, financing, etc. Once you have a good background and understand the lending business, you are ready to proceed. The first step is to begin developing your own "black book" of names of active lenders who will work with you. Develop a file of LOCAL lenders (within your own state) first. Later, you can move on to national firms. It is best to try to get a commission from the LENDER as well as the borrower, if you can. Next, have some simple forms or agreements drawn up by yourself or your lawyer detailing in simple terms that your client (borrower) will pay you a certain fee if you help him obtain his financing. Then obtain a business license, run your ads and you're in business. There will never be any problem in finding borrowers. There will be a screening process to eliminate those firms and individuals who have no chance of obtaining a loan, however. You can take down information over the phone or by mail on a form concerning the assets, liabilities, sales, and other basic information needed, such as the purposes of the loan, etc., and the financial history of the borrower. Stay in contact with your lenders if a good prospective borrower comes up and you'll soon be making money— real money. (It is not unusual for a beginner to make $40,000 net his first year, even operating part-time.)

Earn Money Clipping Newspaper Articles

Earn money clipping newspaper articles by looking in newspapers for stories on people. Many times the names and addresses are included. Clip out the articles and write or call the people in the articles saying you will laminate the article and send it to them for $1. You may be able to have the article laminated locally for a small cost.

Get Unclaimed Money

Every year millions of dollars goes unclaimed and is put in state unclaimed property funds. In most states you can obtain lists of these funds simply by writing to the unclaimed property division and requesting their directory. The newspaper with the largest circulation in your area will also publish this list at least once a year. You can then find the people on the list and inform them that they have money coming to them. Often they have only moved to a different neighborhood or area and can easily be found through the telephone book or by contacting the post office, Department of Motor Vehicles, or county courthouse. For a small finder's fee you can help them recover these funds that are rightfully theirs. You may be able to collect over $2000 per hour if you are able to locate a large account and return it to the rightful owner. An informative book on the subject is **"$2000 an Hour,"** published by Lion Publishing, 6150 Mission Gorge Road, Suite 225, San Diego, CA 92120.

Getting Money By Helping The HUD

When someone takes out a loan to buy or refinance a home, they must have insurance on their loan. The government provides this insurance through the Department of Housing and Urban Development (HUD). Most people pay off their mortgages diligently for thirty years without ever having to default on the loan and collect this insurance. After this amount of time, however, it is easy to forget about the insurance payment which was agreed to so long ago. Many people do not realize that, when the mortgage is paid off, they get this money back!

This is where you can assist HUD as a tracer. HUD always tries to refund these insurance policies, but it is rare these days that someone will stay in the same house for thirty years, and if they cannot be found at the original address, HUD often has no way to find them. If you can track down these policy holders, make them aware of their refunds, and successfully return the money to them, you can collect a percentage of their refund.

There are two HUD programs to work from. One is the Mutual Mortgage Insurance, which is collected as a monthly payment during the life of the loan. This can total as much as nine hundred dollars. The other is the Mutual Insurance Premium, paid as a one-time lump sum when the loan is opened. This is often as much as three-thousand dollars. It is possible for you to collect up to 15% of this money when you return it to the rightful owners.

One book which discusses all the details of this program, as well as explaining methods of finding recipients who have moved, drawing up all the contracts necessary to collect the refunds, and proper avenues of dealing with potential clients, is **"$100,000 Refunds From U.S."** from Lion Publishing. You can get this book by sending $12.95 to them at 6150 Mission Gorge Road, San Diego, CA, 92120.

The $500-A-Month Plan

One of the best ways to make money or start a business of your own is by placing advertisements which will pay a good profit. Selling printed information by mail can be financially rewarding. Classified advertising is the cheapest way to get into mail-order and it is often possible to make a fortune from these small ads. Just check any large publication, such as "Popular Science," for their classified advertising section and you can see for yourself the many ads. These small ads would not be there if they were not profitable moneymakers. You can see the same ads month after month. You can make up to $500 per month or more by running the following classified ads over your name and address. Pick a top national publication and test either one or both under the heading "Money Making Opportunities." Then watch the dollars come in. Here are the advertisements: "How would you like to receive $25 daily and keep all the money? For complete set-up rush $1 to (your name and address)." Fill the orders you receive with a copy of this plan (have them copied by photo off-set, mimeograph, Xerox or whatever). If you study the many classified ads in the big national publications, you may get a better idea of what the leading companies in mail-order are doing. It is truly possible to make money with this plan. Good luck!

You Can Make Money From Your Cable Television

If you watch TV, and pay attention to the advertisements you see there, you probably know as much about

111

commercials as most advertising executives. You know what times are most popular to watch, you know what times the best programs are on, and you know which ads you do and do not like. Why can't you make money in the advertising world like a television executive? Well, maybe you can.

Many products on the market today have the **potential** for phenomenal sales if only they could be promoted properly. You can use your television advertising knowledge to help these products. If you know of a product, perhaps manufactured abroad, which you feel could benefit from a better marketing scheme, you may want to take it to one of the many cable TV marketing firms which specialize in television advertising. For a percentage, they will market your product on cable television and you will benefit from the sales. If you are buying from a firm which will dropship, you may not even have to touch the merchandise. Also, if you want to produce your own advertising video, many cable TV stations will give you free air time in return for a percentage of your total sales. A book from Lion Publishing Co. called **"$1,000,000 Cash Vision"** can tell you who to contact in the world of cable TV to find out about advertising. You can purchase it for $12.95 at 6150 Mission Gorge Rd., #225, San Diego, CA, 92120

Make Money With Your Camera

Most people fail to think about how vulnerable they are to robbery or theft until it happens. Almost everyone has insurance of one type or another, but often this is not enough. If you own a camera, you can help people and make money by taking pictures of valuable items.

You can start a business by offering an "extra insurance program," that is, taking photographs of peoples' valuables (jewelry, furniture, electronics, family heirlooms, etc...) and logging these in some type of file or portfolio.

Insurance companies give special rates to someone who is this conscientious, and police are often able to recover stolen items if they have a physical description to go by. People who hear of this will gladly pay a percentage of the money they save for the service of having valuables photographed for protection.

If you would like more information on this type of business, you will find a book titled **"Thousands Of Dollars A Day With Your Camera"** to be a great source. It is available through Lion Publishing Co., 6150 Mission Gorge Rd., Suite 225, San Diego, CA 92120 for just $12.00.

Make A Fortune Selling Books By Mail

Lion Publishing Company, which has been selling books since 1979, can show you how to make big money selling its nationally advertised books by mail. They give you the books far below wholesale, as well as full-page fliers to promote their line of mail-order and self-improvement books. Many of their books are hard-bound and sell for about $10, which makes them very attractive for mail-order buyers. Write to them about full dealership information: Lion Publishing Company, Mission Gorge Rd., #225, San Diego, CA, 92120.

Section Three

How To Make and Save Money On Your Home and Automobile

How To Get Free Land In Canada

Write to either the Dept. of Land and Forest Parliament Bldg., Quebec City, Canada, or to Communication Group, 2630 Point Grey Rd., Vancouver 8, B.C.

Where To Buy Land At $1.25 An Acre

You can get U.S. Land for only $1.25 an acre if you are willing to irrigate and cultivate up to 320 acres. Get FREE information from U.S. Bureau of Land Management, Washington, D.C., 20240.

How To Buy Homes And Land For A Few Dollars

Yes, you can buy homes, apartments and land for next to nothing by using the procedure of bidding at "tax delinquency and lien sales." These are made to recover unpaid taxes on property which is auctioned off 3 to 4 times each year. Check with your local tax assessor for dates. In the past, people have picked up $50,000 homes for as little as $2,000 and apartments and land for similar discounts.

How To Stop Paying Property Taxes On Your Home

The way to do this is to sign over the title of your home to your nonprofit organization. You can form your own church or organization and apply for the tax-exempt status at your county courthouse. Or, you can sign over the title of your home to your local church or other nonprofit organization if you do not wish for it to go to your heirs. Under this arrangement, you retain lifetime habitation rights although the property belongs to the local nonprofit organization.

Get Expensive Mansion Without Cash

Set up your own corporation by looking for expensive homes for sale, or contact real estate offices. Sign the note for a corporation for a yearly rental—with probable option to buy later—then move in; if the note is for 90 days, you may not have to pay rent—or you can start small monthly payments if necessary. If you want to keep the house and buy it, go to the original owner and offer a lower price than originally mentioned or pay cash for a lower price with stock of corporation for the balance. Get the loan from the savings & loan for the lower price. Another alternative would be to become a "house-sitter." Live in a luxury home for the homeowner who may be away traveling for months. If you live in a large city, you can probably get ALL YEAR FREE RENT by simply "house-sitting" for different homeowners and using names of previous clients as references.

Your Own Home For Just One Dollar

Are there homes and properties in your neighborhood which are abandoned, repossessed, or run-down? If you've contemplated buying and repairing this kind of property, then the government might like to help you with your idea.

The Department of Housing and Urban Development has a program called "Urban Homesteading" which is designed to restore old and dilapidated buildings in needy communities throughout the country. Under this program, homes which have been repossessed by the HUD in areas of poverty are dispersed to needy families who are either from the area, first-time homebuyers, or paying 30% of their total income to housing.

If you meet their qualifications, you may be able to get a low-interest home loan from the government to buy a home. **You may even be able to buy a home for $1.** The only qualification is that you agree to renovate the home that you buy within the first three years that you are living there. You must also agree to live in the home for no less than five years total. After this five year time limit, the government turns title of the home over to you and you may sell the home if you wish. This is a great way to make an unbelievable return on a small initial investment and help to regenerate a needy neighborhood. To find out more about this program, simply contact the Department of Housing and Urban Development in Washington, D.C. If you would like a complete run-down on the program, the book **Getting One Dollar Homes From The U.S. Government** is an excellent publication. You can get it from Lion Publishing Co., at 6150 Mission Gorge Rd., #225, San Diego, CA, 92120. The cost is $10, which may be more than the price of your new house!

How To Buy A Home Inexpensively

The first thing you should do is study the area in which you plan to buy a house and see how the prices run there. Before closing the deal it is always important to have a building inspector check over the structural foundation and mechanical systems of the house. A display of emotional attachment to the house you are looking at ruins all chance of successful negotiations. When you find a home that you really want, walk through the house very quickly. The impression you should give the person showing you the home is that you are quite bored with that home. Mention features or qualities that the house lacks and then indicate that the house would not be suitable for your purposes even if the price was lower. The next step is to send in friends and relatives to look at the property and instruct them to be even more critical of the house's negative features (small yard, lacks the proper facilities, not enough parking, etc.). These relatives and friends make an offer to buy the home 20%-30% below the selling price with a low-interest mortgage and a long settlement date off-setting the selling price of the house. The realtor has to submit to the seller all offers made on the homes. The low offers made by relatives and friends will probably all be rejected by the insulted seller. When the seller's confidence in the home he is selling is diminished, the original buyer comes back to the house to have one more look. Sometimes at this point, the seller will respond favorably to an offer made by this buyer. The buyer can make a low offer for the home and at that point, his offer may be accepted.

Get An Exclusive Office With No Rent

The way to do this is to become a "rental manager." Many office complexes have vacant space because there is no on-the-premises manager to show the space or answer questions. Find out which complexes are having vacancy problems and locate the owner. He will normally be glad to offer you an office if you answer calls and show off the spaces to prospective clients.

Do You Want To Live In Paradise?

In some of the National Forests around the country, ⅓ to ½ acre lots can be leased. Write, specifying the area to which you are interested in relocating, to: U.S. Dept. of Agriculture, Forest Service, Washington, D.C., 20402.

Real Estate Property Disposal

Do you want to buy an inexpensive piece of property? Then get on the list to receive invitations to bid on real estate. Contact: The Property Management and Disposal Service, General Services Administration, 7th and "D" Sts., Washington, D.C., 20407.

Timber And Forest Products: A Good Business To Get Into

Inquire about low cost purchase or lease-acreage in National Forests. Write: Forest Service, Dept. of Agriculture, Washington, D.C., 20400.

Live In A $500,000 Home Without Money

This is the best way is to become a "house-sitter." You offer to live in luxury homes while the owners are away vacationing. If you live in a large city you can probably live all year rent free by keeping a notebook of clients who need your services to protect their homes from vandals while they are away. If necessary, get yourself bonded.

Real Estate

The fact is that the largest percentage of fortunes are made in real estate dealings: land, housing units and commercial buildings. You are aware of the tremendous growth in real estate values in recent years. This trend is almost a certainty to continue. Population growth, and even increased divorce rates create a need for more housing, more business, more recreational areas, etc.

There is no guarantee that all real estate will rise in value during your lifetime, so be selective in what and where to buy. Anticipate the coming trends based on economic, energy and growth factors. Will the population growth be in the outlying areas or will people move back into urban districts? Run-down or semi-abandoned neighborhoods are often profitably renewed. Beautify a house or two in such areas where other people are anxious to do the same. Is an industrial complex or amusement center, which will draw a large number of people going to be planned for the area? If so, smart operators will begin buying property, anticipating that homes and businesses will follow and real estate values will rise. Are you considering buying cheap or unimproved land? Usually, it will produce nothing and cost you taxes, though modest in amount, until you sell the property for profit. But, suppose you could develop it for some income producing benefit like pasture land, farming leases, flora for nurserymen, timber, hunting, camping or a recreation area? Unimproved land should be purchased only with the possibility of developing it for some moneymaking purposes.

Free Government Land

Millions of acres of government land are available, mostly in Western States, at unbelievably low prices. There are possibilities for moneymaking setups such as ranches or resorts. You may even strike it rich with mineral discoveries. For information, write to: Bureau of Land Management, Washington, D.C., 20240.

The GSA often offers vacant or improved land to the public. Also, buildings no longer used by the government, but suitable for warehousing or manufacturing, are offered. These are generally sold by sealed bid and sometimes notices appear in local newspapers. For information about GSA sales write to: General Services Administration, 7th & "D" Streets S.W., Washington, D.C., 20407.

State governments also sell land and property. In some cases they may even give away property which is badly in need of repair or reclamation. Agencies are titled differently in each state, so contact a state office to learn which agency handles land.

Let The Government Pay Your Mining Expenses

Willing to gamble a little to strike it rich with the odds far greater in your favor than winning a state lottery or hitting the giant jackpot in a Las Vegas casino?

Every month, the federal government conducts a lottery for about 1,000 oil and natural gas leases. These are parcels of land ranging from a few acres to 2,500 acres. This land is termed "wildcat" because these areas lie outside the known geological formations that produce gas and oil fields. If an oil company wants to explore your lease it will pay you "up front" money and a royalty for any gas or oil found.

The entry fee is $75. While the procedures are quite simple, an explanation of how the lottery works and how to file requires more space than this report can provide. Write for "Simultaneous Oil and Gas Lease Filings" to Bureau of Land Management, Washington, D.C., 20240.

Cashing In On Repos And Foreclosures

Many agencies of the government collect real estate from borrowers who cannot pay their bills. They, of course, have no use for land holdings, so they must auction them off to the highest bidder. Many people find incredible values at these auctions—homes and land for themselves and to sell for a profit. You can find out about these auctions by contacting government agencies, such as the Veterans Administration or the Department of Housing and Urban Development. Many branches of the government hold these fantastic sales.

One book which is a must for anyone interested in collecting their share of government foreclosed real estate is "Getting Rich With Foreclosures." It costs only $15, and is available through Lion Publishing Co. at 6150 Mission Gorge Road, #225, San Diego, Calif., 92120

How to Get Mortgage Assistance

Those eligible are families and businesses displaced by HUD. programs, low-income families and low credit risk family loans. For more information write to: Federal Housing Administration, Dept. of Housing and Urban Development, 451 7th St., Rm. 3158, Washington, D.C., 20410, or contact your local HUD office

How To Get Free Rent

You can get free rent through one of three methods: 1) Manage an apartment. 2) Be a building caretaker. 3) House-sit. Opportunities to get free rent by all three of these methods may be found simply by checking the classified advertising section of newspapers in the area you wish to live. Most of the opportunities will be listed under the "Help Wanted ads." Managing apartments consists of collecting rents, showing empties, and doing minor repairs such as fixing leaking faucets, replacing lightbulbs and taking care of the grounds. Some untis even pay a small salary depending on the size of the complex. In a very large complex there is usually a separate maintenance man and/or caretaker. The manager only handles collection of the rent and getting the empties occupied. These positions normally pay only a token salary along with the free rent. House sitting is a lot more attractive to the average person. The only drawback is that most opportunities are for short periods, three months to a year at a time. However, if you want to live in an area for a short time, this is the way to do it while living rent-free. Lots of people would rather have someone occupy their home during their absence than have it sit empty. You would be expected to maintain the place and treat it better than if it were your own. For more insight into the business of apartment managing, write to: "Apartment Owners and Managers News", P.O. Box 238, Watertown, Conn., 06795.

Get $20,000 Worth Of Free Furniture

You can obtain free furniture and a lot of other merchandise by starting up a "Freebie Newspaper." Contact store owners and merchants who normally advertise in regular local papers and offer to run their ads in exchange for FREE furniture or other merchandise. True, you will be running their ad free, but chances are you wouldn't have a paid ad for that space either. If you promote this right, you can grow into a large operation and go into PAID circulation before you know it. In the meantime, and for as long as you like, you can continue to receive FREE merchandise in exchange for advertising.

Lawyers' Title Home Buying Guide

This book explains in nontechnical language the process of home buying. This 160-page paperback is available from Lawyers' Title Insurance Corporation, Box 27567, Richmond, Va., 23261, or call (804) 281-6700 for further information.

How To Get Home Financing

The FHA has helped many Americans finance their homes. Write to the FHA for a list of titles of free books that will enable you to choose a home financing plan. For more information, write to: U.S. Dept. of Housing and Urban Development, 451 7th St., Rm. 3158, Washington, D.C., 20410 (or contact your local HUD office).

How To Get A Home Improvement Loan

You may qualify for an improvement loan for your home or apartment building. Any lender participating in the FHA loan insurance program can make applications for such loans. Contact: Federal Housing Administration, Dept. of Housing and Urban Development, 451 7th St., Rm. 3158, Washington, D.C., 20410.

Save On Motel Costs

You can stay at an elegant motel and pay only half the prevailing rate. An American survey has disclosed that a large number of lesser-known motels charge only $10-$13 a night. Over 2200 motels are listed in the new "1987-88 National Directory of Budget Hotels." For a copy, send $3.95 plus $1 postage and handling costs to: Pilot Books, 103 Cooper St., Babylon, N.Y., 11702.

Your Free $495 Automobile Report

One man in Florida is selling this report for $495, but you can have it free! Are you convinced that you will never own a luxury automobile like a Porsche, BMW, or Mercedes-Benz? Well don't give up hope yet. There is a way for you to drive away the car of your dreams and to make lots of money helping others to do the same. **The Gray Market,** which began with the occasional importation of a few European cars by enthusiastic car collectors and returning American servicepeople, is today a thriving "underground" industry.

The gray market involves buying luxury European automobiles, like Porsches, Maseratis, Jaguars, Ferraris, BMWs, and Mercedes-Benz, in Europe where they're manufactured and sold more cheaply. You can save thousands by buying the car of your dreams over there, or make thousands by selling your bargain over here at the upscale prices those cars command. In most cases, the cars need to be modified to meet the stricter American standards, and you will have to pay certain importing and licensing fees, but because of those lower European prices, you can buy your dream car for about a third of what it might cost you to drive it off the lot of some fancy stateside showroom. You can also make a bundle selling these cars to others.

The gray market works because the value of European currency is lower than the American dollar. The dollar has slipped somewhat in recent years, and the spectacular 50% savings possible just a few years ago has been reduced

127

somewhat. Keep in mind, however, that the value of currency runs in cycles, and the amazing savings possible in the "hey day" of the gray market may be only a few months away. Take a look at the deals that are possible:

TYPE OF CAR	DEALER PRICE	YOUR PRICE
Jaguar XJ-6	$44,130	$23,912
Mercedes 300 E	$43,000	$19,484

You either can purchase your automobile in Europe and have it properly modified and licensed yourself, or you can buy it (for a bit more of course) from a stateside automobile broker who is in the business of importing those bargains. They know exactly what steps must be taken to make your car street legal. There is quite a bit involved, but the savings are amazing. Once you know the "ins and outs" you can become a broker and make thousands of dollars importing and selling luxury cars.

The definitive book on this subject is **Gray Market Riches** from Lion Publishing Co., 6150 Mission Gorge Rd., #225, San Diego, CA, 92120. The cost is $19.95.

What To Look For When Buying A Used Car

Examine the framework (chassis), engine block and support for cracks and welding. If cracks or welds are obvious, the car should be passed up. Listen for noises in the motor. Make sure wheels are in proper alignment. Light or heavy bangs or knocks may be due to poor valve adjustment or loose bearings, worn pistons or carbon deposits. Uneven running of the motor may mean distributor trouble, poor spark plugs or improper timing. If the clutch facing is worn, you will experience a jerky starting or the engine may race when going up a grade without showing sufficient power. If, while driving, you hear a bang in the rear end, it may be due to a broken tooth in the master pinion gear in the differential. This will eventually cause more teeth to break and finally stop the car. A broken bearing in the rear wheel is indicated by a heavy thump in the wheel while driving. The steering post can be tested by turning it two inches in either direction. If the wheels do not turn within this space, the steering worms may be worn or there may be loose steering connections. Examine the spring leaves beneath the car to see that none are broken. Make sure the battery is charged and that the generator is charging. The cooling system including the radiator hose and water pump should be examined carefully for leaks. Road test the car at various speeds to see if the motor runs hot. If a sharp click is heard on starting off, and then the noise stops, it may indicate worn universal joints. Check up on this by starting, stopping and reversing. If upon pressing on the starter only a whirring sound is heard it may indicate a broken tooth on the flywheel or that a mesh gear is stuck.

How To Buy A New Car For $50 Over Dealer Cost

You can purchase your next car with the exact optional equipment you want and pick the car up at your local dealer; YET, you will only pay as little as $50 over the dealer cost. The car will be completely guaranteed and serviced just as if you had paid the full retail price. No strings. How? By buying through a reputable new car broker. Check with the brokers in your area for complete information.

Get A Free Cadillac, Mercedes Or Other Fine Luxury Car Every Year

Again, you can work this by having your own nonprofit church or institute furnish you with a vehicle for church work. Under IRS codes, such vehicles can also be used for personal affairs. Still another method is to become an automobile broker for a local dealership. You work out a deal whereby you sell so many cars to your friends, etc., that you are furnished with a NEW car every year in return. I have personally worked this gambit many times.

Section Four

Information You Can Collect

Free Goods And Services

100 Ways To Save Energy & Money In The Home

"Free Home Energy Helper" is a brochure published by the Canadian Dept. of Energy, Mines and Resources. It gives you tips on how you can stretch energy resources and put money in your pocket. This brochure explains the 'whys' and 'hows' of conservation and can be consulted when specific questions arise. By following the ways to save energy and by adopting conservation practices, you can save MONEY in the home. For a free copy, write to: Free Home Energy Helper, 580 Booth St., Rm. 828, Ottawa, Ontario, Canada K1A0E4.

Don't Get Caught Unprepared When Taking Out A Loan

This handy booklet can save you more dollars and it can also decrease the profits at loan coordinators. For a free copy write: Credit Shopping Guide, Federal Trade Commission, D&D Branch, Pennsylvania Ave. at 6th St. N.W., Washington, DC 20580.

Improve Your Home

You can do this on your own and inexpensively. For a free list of plans on home improvement, please write: Ideas for the Home Craftsman, Circulation Manager, Western Wood Products Association, 522 S.W. 5th Ave., Yeon Bldg., Portland, Ore., 97204

Free Information

This is free information for seniors on how to save money in whatever you do. For your free information, write: National Council of Senior Citizens, 1511 K Street N.W., Washington, DC 20005. (202) 783-6850

How To Get Free Subscriptions To Magazines

There are a large number of "Trade" magazines, journals, newsletters, and newspapers which are mailed absolutely FREE to interested firms and individuals who merely ask for them. These are not, of course, the common magazines you find on your local newsstand, but they do offer much valuable reading. To locate the names & addresses of magazines which offer free subscriptions, simply go to the library and ask the librarian for a copy of "Standard Rate & Data." This book lists all trade magazines & specialty publications. It also tells which magazines are "Controlled Circulation," which normally indicates it is free. All you have to do is write the magazine and ask them to place your name on the mailing list. Indicate interest in or some connection with the subject matter of the magazine.

Where To Get Moneymaking Magazines For Free

The following firms give sample copies and sometimes sample subscriptions which contain hundreds of profit opportunities. Write:

"Wealth Secrets That Make Millionaires," 6150 Mission Gorge Road, #225, San Diego, CA, 92120

"Successful Opportunities Magazine," 6150 Mission Gorge Road, #225, San Diego, CA, 92120

"Money Making Opportunities," 11071 Ventura Blvd., Studio City, CA 91604.

"Salesman's Opportunity Magazine," #405, 6 N. Michigan Ave., Chicago, IL 60602.

"Making Profits," 6255 Barfield Rd., Atlanta, GA 30328.

"Spare Time Magazine," 5810 W. Oklahoma Ave., Milwaukee, WI 53219.

How To Get Free Information On Hundreds Of Thousands Of Subjects

The U.S. government publishes thousands of books every year on every subject imaginable. If you want some information on a specific subject, write: Superintendent of Documents, Government Printing Office, Washington, D.C., 20402.

How To Get Free Legal Aid

Low income families can get details about free legal aid by writing to: The Office of Economic Opportunities, Legal Services, Washington, D.C., or, if you live in a large city, consult the Yellow Pages of your phone directory for a local Legal Aid Society.

This Book Is Free

For Americans who want energy independence, write for your free information to: "Energy Independence," 1629 K St. N.W., Suite 500, Washington, D.C., 20006.

Need Money?

This company boasts 2100 loan sources. Write for free details concerning sources that permit you to borrow any amount. Write to Richard Caipo, Diversified Investments, 1231 Cranston St., Cranston, R.I. 02910.

How To Get Free Medical And Dental Care

Once you have formed your own nonprofit organization, as detailed elsewhere, you merely place in your corporate charter the provision that medical care be paid by the organization of which you are a member. The organization, if set up properly, would obtain its money through donations and grants which you would actively seek. Thus, medical care is FREE.

How To Get Free Life Insurance And Pension

Again, as above, you merely include these benefits in your corporate charter so that YOU, as a member or officer of the organization, receive the free benefits from the organization.

How To Get Free Travel

Still again, it is possible to appoint yourself as President of your nonprofit organization and have the organization supply you with a "free" vehicle with all expenses. If your organization is a church-related corporation, you can travel Europe for free—to visit cathedrals, for example. A Church can raise money by "selling" charters, degrees, and other cheap paper for hundreds of dollars. Many nonprofit organizations sell "degrees" and diplomas for upwards of $1,500 each—and it's legal. A good book on the subject is "Make A Fortune And Travel Absolutely Free" is available for $20 through Lion Publishing Co., 6150 Mission Gorge Road, Suite 225, San Diego, CA 92120.

How To Get Thousands Of Books Each Year...Free

One way to do this is to become a book reviewer. You start by convincing a local newspaper to carry a column of book reviews under your name. You can offer your column as a "freebie" to the newspaper on the grounds that many readers would be interested in reading book reviews. Or you can convince a book store to carry your column as part of an ad. Once you become published, send tear-sheets to all major publishers and ask to be placed on their reviewers' mailing list. You will receive a free copy of every new book published.

Discounts of up to 35% on your new book purchases, including those on the best sellers lists, can be obtained from The Book Post, 141 E.44th St., New York, NY 10017. Also from Bookquick, Inc., 160 Eagle Rock, Roseland, NJ 07068.

How To Start Your Own Mailbox Book Club

Book-of-the-month clubs are million-dollar businesses because many people live in rural areas where no library is available. These people purchase from 5-10 books at a time. A Pennsylvania man has started a book club in which people pay a yearly rate of $12 to receive all the books they can read. In addition to the $12 fee, they must also pay postage on all books they receive. When they are finished with the books, they return them to the man so that the books can be sent to other people who wish to rent them. The book club business is operated by the man year-round. He belongs to 10 book clubs himself and originally received his first selections for about $1 for every 5 to 8 books ordered. He started with about 50 to 60 best sellers and then began advertising his own book club. Renting a book is much cheaper than buying one, so your business should do quite well. Suggestion: make a list of all the books you have available and mail your list to interested people who will answer the following classified ad we have prepared for you; "Don't buy books—rent them! List of Top Sellers sent to you for a stamp. (Your name and address)."

How To Travel Anywhere In The World For Free—Two Ways

You can travel anywhere in the world and stay free in private homes or luxury hotels. How? By one or both of the following methods:

Method #1—a Co-Operative Exchange and Travel Club (listed below) for as little as $5. As a travel club member, you receive a list of as many as 5,000 names and addresses from all over the U.S. and the world. Only members receive the list. As a member, you offer your home as a stopping point for compatible people when it is convenient for you. In return, you can stay for free in any of over 5,000 homes throughout the world. Most of the people who belong to these clubs are interesting, adventurous and fun-loving. On your next vacation, enjoy the personal contact of staying in someone else's home. See the world on a shoestring and enjoy! Write to the following club for complete details:

Vacation Exchange Club, 12006 111th Ave., Youngtown Ariz., 85363.

Method #2—an "outside agent" for a travel agency, a tour guide or coordinator for group tours. Go to a large travel agency and contract for a free trip (all expenses paid) in exchange for your securing 20 to 30 people to go with you on a group tour.

How To Get Free Subscriptions To Over 100 Magazines

Instructions: To receive your choice of these free magazines, type your request on your letterhead or on a plain sheet of paper. Ask to be placed on their mailing list to receive future copies. Some of the magazines may arrive only every few months or once a year. In these cases, simply mail another request for the magazine to continue your subscription indefinitely. I have been receiving some of these magazines for almost 10 years by resubmitting my request every six to twelve months. Are you interested in receiving the more popular newsstand magazines? You can't get them free but you can get them wholesale. All you have to do is become a subscription agent. Write to: McGregor Magazine Agency, Mount Morris, Il., 61054. Request the "Wholesale Magazine Subscription Catalog." Many times you can deal directly with a magazine and become one of its subscription agents. "Reader's Digest" is one such magazine. By becoming an agent and subscribing yourself under a business name, you can receive "Reader's Digest" for a discount much below the normal subscription price. (Wholesale rates for businesses are lower than consumer rates).

"Economic Perspective"Federal Reserve Bank of Chicago, P.O. Box 834, Chicago, IL 60690

"Spare Time"—The Kipling Publishing Corp., 5810 W. Oklahoma Ave., Milwaukee, Wi 53219

"Money Making Opportunities"—Success Publishing Co., Inc., 11071 Ventura Blvd., Studio City, CA 91604

"Mineral Industry Surveys"—U.S. Bureau of Mines, Washington, DC 20240

"Business Education World"—Gregg Div., McGraw-Hill Book Co., Princeton Rd. Hightstown, NJ 08520

"Carnation"—Carnation Co., 5045 Wilshire Blvd., Los Angeles, CA 90036

"Today's Office"; "Office World News"—Hearst Publications, 645 Stewart Ave., Garden City, NY 11530

"Business Marketing"—Business Marketing Circulation Dept., 965 E. Jefferson Ave., Detroit, MI 48207

"Export Magazine"—American Exporter and Industrial World, Johnston Publishing, 386 Park Ave. S., New York, NY 10016

"Economic Review"—Federal Reserve Bank of Cleveland, Box 6387, Cleveland, OH 44101

"Directory of Business and Investment Services"—Select Information Exchange, 2095 Broadway, New York, NY 10023

Free Catalogs—Impact Specialty Co., 395 Monroe Circle S., Des Plaines, IL 60016

"Publication and Works in Progress"—Library Research Center, University of Illinois, 220 Armory, Urbana, IL 61820

"Alberta Facts"; "Alberta Statistics Review Quarterly"—Alberta Bureau of Statistics, 7th Floor Sir Frederick W. Haultain Bldg., 9811 109th St., Edmonton, Canada T5K0C8

"Unisys Annual Report"—605 3rd Ave., New York, NY 10158

"The Freeman"—Foundation for Economic Education, Inc., Irvington on Hudson, NY 10533

"PPG Products"—Kathleen Smith, PPG Industries, 1 PPG Place, Pittsburgh, PA 15272

"Canada Today"—Canadian Embassy, Office of Information 1771 N. St., N.W., Washington, DC 20036

"Ward's Bulletin"—Ward's Natural Science Establishment, Inc., P.O.Box 92912, Rochester, NY 14692

"Rural Living"—(free to Co-op members) Virginia Association of Electric Cooperatives, P.O. Box 15248, Richmond, VA 23227

"Modern Office Technology"—1100 Superior Ave., W., Cleveland, OH 44117

"Consol News"—Consolidated Coal Co., Consol Plaza, Pittsburgh, PA 15241

"New York-France-New York"—French Cultural Services, 40 W. 57th St., Ste 2100, New York, NY 10019

"IFCO News"—Inter-Religious Foundation for Community Organization, 402 W. 145th St., New York, NY 10037

"Conservation News"—(depends on membership)— National Wildlife Federation, 8925 Leesburg Pike, Vienna, VA 22181

"Marathon World"—Marathon Oil Co., 539 S. Main St., Findlay, OH 45840

"Bulletin"—Chevron Oil Co. of California, 225 Bush St., San Francisco, CA 94120

"Friend's"; "Chevy Outdoors"—30400 Vandyke, Warren, MI 48093

"National Economic Trends" (plus six other publications, ask for the list)—Federal Reserve Bank of St. Louis, Box 442, St. Louis, MO 63166

"Gold Bulletin"—Chamber of Mines, 5 Holland St., Johannesburg, South Africa

"Memo To Mailers"—U.S. Postal Service, "Memos to Mailers", Washington DC., 20260

"Brazil"; "Brazilian Bulletin"—Brazilian Government Trade Bureau, 551 5th Ave., New York, NY 10017

"Steinway News"—John Steinway, Steinway and Sons, Steinway Place, Long Island, NY 11105

"School Product News" (for school employees)—School Products News, 1100 Superior Ave., Cleveland, OH 44114

"Lawn Care"—Scotts, 14111 Scotts Lawn Rd., Marysville, OH 03041

Bimonthly Bulletins available—Information Div., Dept. of External Affairs, L.B. Pearson Bldg.—Domestic Comm. Div. (BFC), Tower C, 2nd Floor, 125 Sussex Dr., Ottawa, Ont., K1A0G2

"Sun"—Sun Oil Co., Corporate Public Relations, Karen Higgins, 100 Matsonford Rd., Radnor, PA 19087

"Norelco Reporter"—Philips Electronic Instruments, 750 S. Fulton Ave., Mt. Vernon, NY 10050

"California Agriculture"—Mr. Dick Venne, Editor, CA Agriculture, 2120 University Ave., Floor 7, UC Berkeley, Berkeley, CA 94720

"Old News is Good News"—Utah Division of Aging and Adult Services—120 N. 200 W., Salt Lake City, UT 84102

"Creative Ideas In Glass"—ASG Industries, Inc., Marketing Dept. c/o Mariann Decker, P.O. Box 929, Kingsport, TN 37662

"Pakistan Affairs"—Embassy of Pakistan, 2315 Massachusetts Ave., N.W., Washington D.C. 20008

"E.G.& G Inc."—E.G.& G. Inc., 45 Williams St., Wellesley, MA 02181

Government Surplus

Vehicles, office equipment, and boats are among many thousands of goods the government sells at a small fraction of their value. As requirements change, large quantities of goods became obsolete by government specifications and are classed "surplus," then offered to the general public.

If you buy something at a real bargain price and resell it for a high profit, you have made big money on the deal. Some items can be bought at as low as **2 cents on the dollar.** While many of these items can be bought and profitably resold to various markets, an imaginative idea or application could make you rich! A case in point is a fellow named Hugh Paulk who bought 50,000 surplus parachutes, a few at a time, and sold them by mail at $13.95 each. Did he sell them to airplane clubs, sky divers or private pilots? No. He advertised in women's magazines and they were quickly grabbed up as fine nylon material

143

for shirts, blouses and other clothing—to the tune of $800,000 sales for Mr. Paulk!

Look through your Yellow Pages and find the Government Surplus dealers in your area. An excellent book on the subject of government benefits and auctions is Cashing In On Government Surplus. This book is available for $14.95 from Lion Publishing Co. at 6150 Mission Gorge Road, #225, San Diego, CA, 92120.

Great Ideas And Secrets

How To Make Your Own Home Brew

This report is presented as information only. The author is not responsible if this recipe is so pleasing that you drink the brew excessively. The necessary ingredients are usually available from most markets, and the bottle capper and caps may be found at most hardware stores. You will also need a crock, about 10 gallons and a hydrometer of the type designed for brewing. The purpose of the hydrometer is to determine when the sugar content for the mix is less than 1%. It will float on top of the mix for about 3 or 4 days, and when it sinks you are ready to bottle the brew. You will need a collection of empty bottles—the quart size is best. Be sure they are completely clean. Ingredients: Malt—2 cups, sugar—5 cups, yeast—1 tbs., water—3 gallons. For a darker color, add more malt. For stronger flavor, add more sugar and a small amount of brewer's hops. The BEST flavor, at least to the author, is to use 3 cups of superfine sugar and 3 cups of brown sugar. This gives about 18% by volume-36 proof. Heat about 2 quarts of water and dissolve the malt syrup. Add the sugar to the mix slowly and stir until it is dissolved. Let the mix boil for several minutes, then pour into crock and add the balance of water. If you use hops, wrap them in cheese cloth and hang them in the mix. Wait about three hours and skim off the foam. Place the hydrometer in the mix and from this point on keep your eye on it. It will sink in about three days or so and you are ready to bottle. The best way to bottle is to use a small siphon hose. Try NOT to disturb the mix. Slowly place the hose about one inch from the bottom and start the siphon action. As each bottle is filled about one inch from the top, pinch the hose to stop the flow and then release and fill the next bottles and let the brew age—at least 10 days, but 30 days is better. The very best flavor comes after about 3 months. If you are smart—start another batch immediately as you will want to start drinking the first one right away. And remember—Don't Blame Me If You Drink Too Much!

Bad Investments

COMMODITIES—This market isn't as good as it seems. It is just a form of gambling in which more than 80% of those who participate lose.

GOLD—Many companies offer you gold-buying plans. The deal consists of a buyer who puts a deposit on the gold he is to receive. This type of deal is very shaky because the cost of the gold contract is more than the money needed to buy a gold future. Another problem with this deal is that small amounts of gold are harder to sell than large amounts of gold.

COINS—As an investor in coins, knowing the current prices and comparison shopping are very important. You will probably pay less at a coin dealership than you would pay for coins through the mail. Coins are a good investment if you know what you are doing.

TAX SHELTERS—Tax shelters can be a bad investment for investors who get the bulk of their income as salary. This type of tax deduction is only a postponed liability that could come up later unexpectedly. The liability isn't worth the risk.

BUYING A UNIT SHARE OF AN INVESTMENT—When buying a unit share of an investment, it is important to note that the smaller the share of the investment you buy, the worse the investment is overall. When a small unit of a large investment is bought, a large percentage of the investment is promoters' fees, management fees, compensation fees, etc. The greater your share of an investment, the more it is worth. Therefore, a 20% share of an investment is worth more than twice a 10% share.

Insurance Tips

1) If you have installed a fire or burglar alarm or a smoke detector in your home, as a home-owner, you are entitled to an insurance deduction.

2) Buying car insurance through a mail order insurance company is usually cheaper than buying car insurance through an insurance agent. The name of one such mail-order company is: Wausau Insurance Companies. 11975 Westline Drive, St. Louis, MO 63141.

3) Never buy travel insurance at the airport. The same insurance coverage is cheaper if you buy it through an independent insurance agent.

4) The cost of medical expenses could be greater than your insurance coverage. A solution is to get an insurance policy that is equal to the maximum coverage under your present insurance policy.

5) Rather than buying medical insurance, there are many advantages in joining a health maintenance organization (HMO). The HMO medical coverage covers most sickness and accident expenses, usually with no deductible. The HMO program emphasizes preventative health care, long-term diagnosis and regular checkups for its members. An HMO program can give you great medical coverage at a good savings.

How Never To Be Without A Job

I made this discovery in California, but the situation is probably true in all areas of the United States. After working for several years in a dead-end job, I quit and found myself without a job and with no idea what I wanted to do. I scanned the ads. One read "Fry Cook Wanted." I once owned a tiny hamburger joint, so I thought, "Maybe I'll try it. I might have enough experience." I phoned the firm. The owner did everything but beg me to take the job. Not once did he ask me about my experience. I took the job. The pay was small but I enjoyed the work. I saw another one offering more money, advertised as a "full-fledged" cook. In about one month, another ad offering $4 per hour (that was in 1970)—word of mouth opportunity—advertising for a head cook, with $700 salary per month. Then, a manager job opened, with $1,200 per month salary. All this happened to me within 1 year—and I started with the ability to fry hamburgers and nothing else. Shortage of cooks? I don't know. All I know is that it's practically impossible for a restaurant to find or keep a cook. I have seen high school boys hired in as dish washers and in two weeks, start as a cook. How can one learn to cook? Make no mistake about it—you don't need to know HOW to cook. Buy an egg pan and learn to flip eggs. This ability alone will get you a job. You don't have to be a cook—just say you are and you'll never, never be without a job.

How To Sell Your Ideas For Huge Royalties

Here is a way to cash-in on your ideas. If they are unique, some company just may be willing to pay big bucks for them. This report explains how to protect your ideas to make sure you get paid for them. Your salable ideas can be something tangible or intangible. Ideas include such things as mechanical things, chemical compounds, design, works of art, advertising and business plans, ideas for improving a design, flavor, etc., of an existing product or service. Many thousands of dollars are paid out to idea men each year by industries. If your idea will increase production, increase sales or improve the product, they will be willing to pay substantial money for it. First, you must know how to "protect" the ideas you generate. Ideas that are made public by word of mouth or even in writing become public property unless you first make an agreement to retain all right to your ideas. Let's say you have an idea for increasing the sales of an existing product for company A. Write it a letter similar to this one in duplicate:

Gentlemen: I have developed a new idea for increasing the sales of your product. This new method will not increase your costs in any manner. If you are interested in the full details, I will forward them to you upon receipt of the below signed agreement. AGREEMENT TO REVIEW IDEA. We, the undersigned, agree to receive in confidence full details about an idea for increasing the sales of Widgets as submitted by (your name). It is further understood that we assume no responsibility whatsoever with respect to features which can be demonstrated to be already known to us. We also agree not to divulge any details of the idea submitted without permission of (your name) or to compensation to be fixed by negotiation with (your name). It will be reviewed in confidence and within a 30 day period we will report to (your name) the results of our findings and will advise whether or not we are interested in negotiating for the purchase of the rights to use said idea.

Have the company sign both copies and return one to you. Then you must submit complete details of your idea to the company. After the company reviews your idea, it must, by law, follow the instructions of the agreement. Many idea men are earning substantial money following this procedure. The sky is the limit, but make darn sure that you get the agreement signed prior to disclosing your idea. Otherwise, no go! To increase chances of having ideas accepted, spend a lot of time preparing complete, minute details before you submit them. This is the key! Include illustrations or drawings if it's necessary to get the story across.

How To Get Free Oil For Your Car

The secret of getting oil for your car absolutely free, or at just pennies per gallon, is to realize that oil does not wear out, it just gets dirty. Remove the dirt and other particles from the oil and it will be like new. It will have all the lubricating qualities it had when new. To make old oil like new: Boil 4 gallons of old oil. Add I pint of liquid silicate of soda. Stir for 10 minutes, let it settle until the oil is clear. Remove the oil from the top. (Sediment and sludge will be at the bottom—avoid tipping the container to such an extent as to stir up the sediment). To get old oil FREE: Go to the local filling stations and ask for their old oil. Usually you can have it for hauling it away. If you plan to sell oil to others, offer to pay the station owner or manager 5 cents a gallon for the oil. Furnish them with a steel drum to put the oil in. This will assure you of a steady supply.

Expanding your business: Hillyard Corporation, 100 W. 4th St., Elmira, NY 14902 has automatic equipment that reclaims oil if you decide to develop your business on a larger scale. Send for their free catalog. You might even consider renting garage space (there are many abandoned gas stations these days) and specialize in oil changes for a buck or two. With oil prices at $1 a quart, it won't take long for you to build a fantastic business.

How To Copyright Any Publication Without Cost

To establish a copyright you must simply print the following notice, either on the cover or the page immediately following the cover in your book, report, etc. Here it is: copyright 1985 John Doe. Most people do not know that you are NOT required to register the copyright with the copyright office. But if you wish to register it, write for the necessary application form. You then submit two copies of the publication along with the application form for each copyright. For necessary forms and additional information, write: Register of Copyrights, Library of Congress, Washington, DC 20559.

How To Vanish And Start Over Again Under A New Identity

Many people change their identity each year for a variety of reasons, sometimes legal, sometimes illegal. The idea is to obtain a "birth certificate" of a deceased individual who would have been your approximate age, hair color, eye color, etc.—had they lived. Preferably, this should be the name of a child, not an infant, at least one year old when he died, and no more than 5 years old, if possible. Search through the death records at your local county or state courthouse. The death records will tell you the name of the parents and other information which is needed to apply for (your) birth certificate. Once you obtain the birth certificate, you can obtain any other official documents almost at will.

If you want more detailed information on changing your identity, you should get in touch with Eden Press, Box 8410, 16681 Evergreen Circle, Fountain Valley, CA 92708. (714) 556-2023. They have one particular book entitled "The Paper Trip," which is quite helpful.

There Is Safety In Patent Numbers

It can cost thousands of dollars in legal fees and other expenses to secure a patent. However, for about $60 an inventor can file a 'disclosure document' with the U.S. patent and trademark office. This procedure will protect the patent for 2 years, while the patent is being worked on. The document is destroyed if no patent is filed at the end of two years.

Cutting And Drilling Glass

The following is a description of how to cut glass without a diamond cutter.

Method #1: First, dip a piece of common string in alcohol and squeeze it as dry as it will get without dripping. This string should then be placed on the already marked glass and tied tightly. Light the string and let it burn off. Immediately, while the glass is still hot, plunge it into cold water. Be sure the container of water is large enough to let the glass go completely under as well as your arm up to the elbow so as to deaden the vibration when you strike the glass. Using a stick of wood and hitting a sharp stroke, strike the glass with your other hand outside the line of cutting. This quick, sharp stroke will break the glass where it has been weakened by the burning string into a clean cut as if done by a regular glass cutter. This method may be used to cut bottles in any shape and to make vases.

Method #2: Here is a method that rarely fails to break glass cleanly. First, scratch the glass with the corner of a file or sharp graver. Have a piece of wire bent to the desired shape you want to cut the glass. Heat the wire to red-hot, and lay it upon the scratch. Sink the glass into cold water just deep enough to come on a level with the wire, not quite covering it. The glass will break clean.

Method #3: (Cutting glass with scissors). To do this you must place the glass under water completely, then, with a pair of ordinary scissors, proceed to cut the glass as you would cut paper or cloth. This method, of course, is not as smooth a job as the methods described above. The edges will not be as smooth, but to get a piece of glass down to size, this method will be satisfactory.

Method #4: Drilling glass. Get a piece of steel wire and file to the shape of a drill. This must be tempered as follows: Heat the end of the drill on a flame until it is dull red, then place in metallic mercury. The drill, tempered in this manner, will bore through glass as if it were drilling through soft metal. When using it in glass, always use oil or turpentine with a little camphor added to lubricate the drill. As you drill, be careful not to drill clear through from one side as you will break the glass this way. Drill almost through, then start from the opposite side and finish the hole. Or, if you cannot do this, as when you are drilling bottles, etc., fill the bottle with water or place the glass in water. Caution: When you make the drill, do not make the cutting edges too sharp or too acute. The drill will cut slowly but you will have better holes with less breakage.

Bonus: Rainbow colors for bottles, vases, etc.—Use floating art colors, available at most paint stores. Take a pail and fill it with water and drop a few drops of several different art colors on top of the water. Now take any article you wish colored and dip it down through the colors, slowly, back and forth. You now have a rainbow colored article. You can color bottles, vases, candles and many more articles in this way.

Project Your TV Image Onto A Screen

The screen used to display the image projected by the TV can be made out of any material or substance that displays a solid white color. The entire projecting device should be encased in wood. The image is projected on to a screen with the use of two convex lenses. The two convex lenses will produce a better picture if they are achromatic. If your TV size is large or smaller than 15", then substitute your TV size into the following formula: [your TV size] x 10" divided by 15". The new value obtained should be substituted for the number below marked with an asterisk. If the focal length of your first lens is larger or smaller than 1", then let 'z' represent the focal length of the first lens. If the focal length of the second lens is larger or smaller than 1", then let 'y' represent the focal length of the lens. (e.g., if focal length $=2$", then $4z = 4(6$") $=24$"). Remember, if you had to substitute any numbers, the new measurements must be applied to the specifications of the TV projector.

The Production Of Gasohol And Alcohol

Alcohol is formed through the process of fermentation of starches and sugars. The mixture of 10% alcohol with 90% gasoline is gasohol. The whole process of producing gasohol requires the production of alcohol. The following procedure is how alcohol is produced from grains. The grains are first allowed to sprout (soak in water for about one week) then they are dried. The grain is crushed, boiled in water for one hour and then the water is strained out. My recipe is 12 parts water to 1 part crushed grain with 7 tsp. of yeast. Stir completely and ferment for about a week. The foam that builds up should be removed. The mixture should be covered (not tightly) for about a week or longer. The grain mixture must be washed by removing the fermented material from the crushed grain. The watery mixture that was separated from the crushed grain should then be distilled. Distilling is the boiling of the fermented mixture. The distilling procedure should be done about 3 times to produce a 95% alcohol (approx.) mixture, which is suitable for gasohol. Note: This report is written as informative information to its readers. Putting this information into practice is illegal. The U.S. liquor law prohibits unauthorized distilling.

Become a Collector

Investors or collectors who deal or trade in items that will multiply in value make big money. Some of the items that have jumped in value through the years are gems (which can be obtained from foreign producers), coins, stamps, old magazines and comic books, baseball trading cards, dolls and toys, rare books, paintings, sculptures, art objects, phonograph records, autographs, guns, etc. Always check current values; buy only at a lower price. And, don't throw out everything your spouse considers trash. A piece of today's junk might be someone's treasure tomorrow.

Thousands Of "Freebies"

Robert and Linda Kalian have researched all over the country and compiled the information in a highly recommended book: "A Few Thousand of the Best Free Things in America." You can order it from Lion Publishing Co., 6150 Mission Gorge Rd. #225, San Diego, CA 92120.

Sell Hobby Items By Mail

You can, if you are ambitious, start a Mail-Order Business selling collectibles to hobbyists by mail. To begin, you must find a hobby that appeals to YOU. Next, you must spend several weeks researching that hobby. You must learn what collectors want and how much they are willing to pay for it. You should also know what other dealers are willing to pay for the merchandise which they sell. And you must be willing to pay the same amounts.

Perhaps you already know exactly what you want to sell. If you have been collecting old Valentines, then start a mail-order business buying and selling old Valentines. You may want to sell stamps, or maybe comic books. The first rule of mail-order selling is to sell what you yourself would buy.

To give you an idea of what collectors buy and sell by mail, here is a partial list of today's collectibles.

Phonograph records	Street car tokens	Boat photographs
Cigar Labels	Fruit Jar Labels	Advertising Cards
License Plates	Old Magazines	Dog Pictures
Beer Labels	Gun Catalogues	Movie Magazines
Circus Posters	Paper Currency	Autographs
Music Boxes	Cartoon Books	Dolls
Salt/Pepper Shakers	Theater Programs	Hunting Licenses
Greeting Cards	Political Buttons	Valentines
Oil Pencils	Baseball Cards	Cookbooks
Atlases	Children's Books	Beatles Items
Military Medals	Stock Certificates	Stamps
Sheet Music	Old Toys	Indian Relics
Doll Cloths	Gems, Minerals	Railroad Books
Menus	Belt Buckles	Fishing Licenses
Cigar Boxes	Airplane Photos	Comic Books
Train Photos	FBI Posters	Thimbles
Old Calendars	Newspapers	Automobile Manuals
Maps	Coins	Diaries
Postcards	Arrowheads	Antique Barbed Wire
Buttons	Old Jewelry	Railroad Passes

I would suggest that you send for sample copies of two magazines. They are read avidly by hobby dealers and hobby collectors alike.

"The Collectors News", (sample copy—$2), Box 156 Grundy Center, IA 50638

"The Antique Trader Weekly", (sample copy—free), Box 1050, Dubuque, IA 52001

Each of these publications contains around 70 or 80 pages of ads from dealers and collectors.

Once you have selected your field, start a file. Keep copies of all the ads selling your kind of merchandise. Also keep ads showing the dealer's buying prices. If price lists are offered in ads, send for them and study them. Make yourself an expert in your field!

Try to locate any publications that deal with your field. Often, you can locate small mimeographed publications and newsletters which will give you all kinds of useful information.

Your next step is to look for merchandise in your own community. Here are some suggestions:

- Start by attending flea markets and antique shows. Don't be afraid to make inquiries of dealers. They often have what they consider 'junk' stashed away, assuming that it isn't of much value to anyone. I once discovered a fabulous stamp collection that way!

- Browse around through thrift shops.

- Study the garage sale ads in your local newspaper. Visit any that sound promising. (Sometimes, it pays to telephone first. Also, by telling people what kind of merchandise you are looking for, they may be able to direct you to others who have exactly what you need!)

- Place "Want to Buy" ads in your local 'Swapper's News', or your local newspaper. Be sure to list your phone number.

It is amazing what you can find in your local community if you work at it. However, if you can't find enough merchandise locally, run ads in the Collector's Magazines listed above. Their rates are very, very low. And you will soon discover that they are widely read.

Once you have accumulated a decent stock of merchandise, you are ready to begin selling it. If there are publications specializing in your field, by all means advertise there. You have a ready-made audience! Also run ads in the big hobby magazines.

Type up a list of what you have, and have an instant printer make a hundred or so copies for you. Hobbyists don't mind typewritten, mimeographed, or Xeroxed copies. It's half the fun of collecting. Then run your ad. Your ad can merely offer your list to interested collectors free (or for a stamp, to weed out coupon clippers). Or you can offer to make a sale straight from the ad. If you do the latter, stick in your price list with the merchandise. It will be read...eagerly!

Here are a few sample ads run by hobby dealers for your consideration:

- "Railroad Timetables, 1940s
  Four different—$4.00 postpaid."

- "Old Childrens' Books and Texts.
  Stamp for List."

- "85,000 Comic Books, Movie Magazines,
  Funnies, etc. 1900-1957, Catalogue

$1 (Refundable)."

- "Original Movie Posters, Pressbooks, Stills, 1919-1975. Catalogue—.50 cents."

- "Sleigh Bells! Stamp for List."

- "Fifteen Tobacco Labels—$3"

- "Sheet Music. SASE for List."

Just in case you are not familiar with the phrase "SASE" it means "Self-addressed, stamped envelope." Most hobby dealers will tell you that they learn more from the collectors who buy from them than they could ever learn from any other source.

Below are some other hobby publications that might interest you. Unless I have listed the sample copy price, it would be a good idea to include postage when requesting copies from the publisher.

"Antiques and Collecting Hobbies", 1006 S. Michigan Ave., Chicago, IL 60605 ($2/copy—available in most libraries.)

"Western Stamp Collector", Box 10, Albany, OR 97321 ($1/copy).

"Linn's Stamp News", Box 29, Sidney, OH 45365 (It is published weekly and is THE stamp collector's paper.) Subscriptions run $25/year, or about 47 cents/copy.

"Doll Castle News", P.O.Box 247, Washington, NJ 07887 ($2.50).

"Canadian Hobby Shopper", Box 3382, Halifax South, NS, Canada B3J 3J1.

Selling Recipes by Mail

During the past few years, a number of very enterprising housewives (and a few men!) have established very successful businesses selling recipes by mail.

The idea is very basic. You create a new recipe and then you advertise it in the classified section of a magazine or newspaper which is read primarily by housewives. You advertise your favorite recipe for a dollar, and some dealers also request a self addressed, stamped envelope. When your receive orders in the mail you mail them a typewritten or Xeroxed copy of your recipe. Even handwritten copies are permissible, if the handwriting is legible. Along with your recipe, include a list of additional recipes you have for sale. The list should tie in with your original offer.

Let us imagine that you have advertised a secret recipe for Danish Butter Cookies. Your list should include other cookie recipes, as well as Danish recipes. If your customer bakes your Danish Butter Cookies and likes them, she will be in a good frame of mind to purchase MORE recipes from you.

In researching this article, I combed through the classified sections of dozens of magazines studying recipe ads. Here is a partial list of recipes that were being sold by mail:

Four Fabulous Christmas Cookies
Delicious Frosted Brownies
Tempting Chocolate Pie (Superb Crust, Topping, Filling!)
Hungarian Green Bean Soup
Delicious Old Fashioned Nut Roll
Famous Pastry Shop Cheesecake
Russian Tea Cakes
Easy Sourdough Starter
Light Moist Coconut Cake
Unique Plum Pudding
Sugarless Diet Desserts
Old Testament Scripture Cake
Coldwater Dill Pickles
High Protein Diet Candy
Polish Recipes
Grandma's Old Fashioned Bread

You will notice a lot of regional and national recipes. If you could collect recipes from a specific country, say Finland, Czechoslovakia, Yugoslavia, etc., they would probably sell very will. Also recipes from New England, the Deep South, or some other special area would do well. Notice the number of recipes that contain words like DELICIOUS, TEMPTING and EASY!, and recipes which are sugarless, or which feature vegetarian specialties, would also do very well.

Many housewives pay a great deal of attention to HOLIDAY recipes. If you can time your ad so that it appears about thirty days before Valentine's Day, St. Patrick's Day, Easter, Mother's Day, 4th of July, Father's Day, Halloween, Thanksgiving, or Christmas...you will do very well selling Holiday recipes.

Where Do You Find The Recipes?

Start by selling your own recipes. Ask your friends if they have recipes that you can use. Often they will be delighted to help you! Or you can go to the library and search through OLD newspapers and magazines. When you find recipes that look promising, go home and experiment with them. WRITE THEM IN YOUR OWN WORDS...otherwise you would be violating copyright laws.

In my research, I discovered the names of two housewives who have made it their business to create new recipes and then sell them to dealers. If you can't create any new recipes to sell, they will create them for you! Here they are:

ADDIE'S RECIPE BOX, 2670 Jackson, Eugene, OR 97405. Addie will send you complete details about her unique business for 35 cents. She has a list of recipes which you can copy to send to your customers. I looked at her list and at the moment she was offering Maple Nut Bars, Polish Apple Rolls, Peppermint Candy Cake, Pineapple Honey Bread, Glazed Strawberry Cake, Giraffe Cut-Up Cakes, etc. It will pay you to contact her!

MRS. WARREN WATSON, Box 9578, Seattle, WA 98109. As I understood it, her husband is a professor who dabbles in the mail-order business on the side, and she became interested in recipe selling. She will tell you all about it if you will send her a self-addressed, stamped envelope.

To get an idea of what kind of recipes are currently being sold, it would be advisable to study the recipe section on the classified pages of the National Enquirer for several weeks. (Their advertising rates are sky-high, but they sell about four million copies of the magazine every week. I notice some of the same ads in every week, and they couldn't continue unless they were getting stacks of orders!)

Below is a list of other publication which carry recipe sections in their classified pages. The list is by no means exhaustive. If you will write to these publications and tell them you are interested in selling recipes by mail, they will send you sample copies and their rate cards.

These are not absolutely up-to-date rates, and of course when the postal rates go into effect, most of these publications will probably raise their rates, so PLEASE CONTACT THE MAGAZINES BEFORE PLACING YOUR ADS.

"CAPPER'S WEEKLY", 616 Jefferson, Topeka, KS 66607. This is a small town farm paper. It sells about half a million copies weekly. $1.20/word, less if you order more insertions at one time.

"NATIONAL ENQUIRER", Lantana, FL 33464. $5.60 per word, four million copies sold weekly mostly to lower and middle-income housewives, recipes probably sell like hotcakes here!

"FARMER", 1999 Shepard Rd., St. Paul, MN 55116. Over two million circulation. 60 cents/word, minimum 15 words.

"THE WOODBASKET", 4251 Pennsylvania Ave., Kansas City, MO 64111. Three million housewives read this one! $6.50/word.

"HBJ FARM PUBLISHING", 120 W. 2nd St., Duluth, MN 55802, ATTN: Sandy Ollah. This company publishes five farm magazines (Kansas, Michigan, Ohio, Pennsylvania, and Missouri).

"PROGRESSIVE FARMER", Box 2581, Birmingham, AL 35202. Has a large farm circulation. $2.55/word. ATTN: Joe Wade.

"GRIT", 208 W. 3rd St., Williamsport, PA 17701. School boys in small towns sell this every week to over a million housewives. $1.80/word; less if you order more insertions at once.

YE OLDE AND NEW COLLECTION OF HINTS, IDEAS, FORMULAS HOME, HEALTH, SEWING, CLOTHING, CLEANING, AND PRODUCTS

Health, Relaxation, Formulas, Hints

1. Try a cup of baking soda in a tub of warm water. Relax for ten minutes or until refreshed.

2. One tablespoon of baby oil in very warm bath water for smooth skin. Watch the wrinkles go.

3. Try a warm bath with feet propped up high for a relaxing twenty minutes.

4. Mix dry oatmeal and water into a paste and spread on face. Lie down and let it dry. Wash off with warm water. Excellent facial.

5. Cold Cream on eyelashes and brows keeps soap out of eyes while shampooing.

6. For that Bright-Eyed look, place cucumber slices on eyelids while relaxing in a hot bath for ten minutes.

7. Remove gum from hair with nail polish remover, then shampoo.

8. Cornbread mix spread on face, let dry and wash off with warm water and see how clean your skin looks.

9. Another refresher...squeeze cotton pads out of ice water, place on eyelids and lie down, elevate feet.

10. To prevent hair pins from falling out, bend one prong in a "V" about halfway up and insert in hair. It will stay.

11. Clean your rings with toothpaste and old brush.

12. Art gum eraser will clean bone colored shoes.

13. To keep Cold Cream from spoiling and maintain its freshness, keep it in the refrigerator.

14. Prevent wrinkled scarves. Roll and place in toilet cones.

15. Old lipstick tubes, thoroughly cleaned, are great for purse-sized pill boxes or for pins, etc.

16. White shoe polish will keep a cast clean on broken bones.

17. Clip on earrings can be used for cufflinks or scatter pins.

18. Cuticle remover will clear hands of nicotine stains.

19. Ice water and soap to remove ring from swollen finger.

20. Cut legs of old card table, to about ten inches high. This will make a good table for sick or bed-ridden folks.

21. Boil pine splinters and sip tea to stop hiccups of long duration.

22. Use a lazy susan at bedside to enable sick to reach more items.

23. Old socks worn over shoes helps prevent falls on ice.

24. Tape on shoes helps prevent falls on highly waxed floors.

25. Emergency sinus relief—swab white vinegar high up in the nostrils.

26. Recycle your own paper—Use backs of unwanted advertising mail for scratch paper pads. Roll your newspapers into a tight roll until they are log size, tie with a wire and burn in the fireplace. It will burn like a log, but even longer. Shred all of your newspapers and junk mail and save in a large bag for use in packing materials and for making paper mache items by adding flour and water.

27. Save cans to freeze leftovers in.

28. Save plastic bags from bread for freezer use.

29. Save plastic milk containers, fill with water and freeze. Use in camper iceboxes or coolers. Also, these can be used to freeze colored water or juices in for later use in a punch bowl.

30. Clean vinyl with liquid window cleaner.

31. Avoid tears when peeling onions, slice first, then slip the bands of skin off.

32. Use an egg slicer to slice apples or mushrooms.

33. Leftover pancake batter makes good fried onion rings. Separate and let soak in batter for fifteen minutes. Fry in hot oil.

34. Loose door knob? Put a drop of shellac in the screw hole, then tighten. It works!

35. To grow thyme—thyme will grow anywhere, but it prefers a dry, poor soil. If the ground is rich, the plant will become too luxuriant and lose its aromatic qualities.

36. Very strengthening drink—beat the yolk of a fresh egg with a little sugar, add a very little brandy, beat the white to a strong froth, stir it into the yolk, fill up the tumbler with fresh milk and grate in a little nutmeg.

37. Cancer cure (for information only)—Take the blossoms of red clover and make a tea of them. Drink freely. This will supposedly cure cancer of the stomach as well as on the surface.

38. How to preserve flowers and fruit—Fruit and flowers may be preserved from decay and fading by immersing them in a solution of gum arabic and water two or three times, waiting a sufficient time between each immersion to allow the gum to dry. This process covers the surface of the fruit with a thin coat of gum, which is entirely impervious to the air, thus preventing the decay of the fruit or flower. Roses thus preserved have all the beauty of freshly picked ones, though they have been separated from the parent stock for many months.

39. Household cleaner formula—Soap powder-2 oz., Soda ash-3 oz., Tri-Sodium Phosphate-40 oz., finely ground silica-55 oz. Mix well and put up in containers. Most of the above items can be purchased from drug stores or hardware and paint stores.

40. Household window cleaner formula—Castile soap-2 oz., water-5 oz., chalk-4 oz., French-chalk-3 oz., Tripoli powder- 2 oz., petroleum spirits-5 oz. Mix well and pack in tight containers. The above ingredients can be purchased at local drug, hardware, paint, or nursery stores.

41. Fire kindler formula—rosin or pitch-10 oz., sawdust-10 or more oz. Melt, mix and cast in forms.

42. Paint brush cleaner—Ammonia (household ammonia will do).

43. Sun burn lotion—Peanut oil (buy at the grocery store).

44. Radiator cleaner—Tri-Sodium Phosphate (buy at the paint store).

45. Tree wound dressing-Lanolin (buy at the drug store).

46. Frosted window paint (super saturated solution of Epsom Salts).

47. Mosquito Repellent—Oil of Pennyroyal, rub on skin. (Buy at the drug store).

48. Furniture polish and cleaner—Vinegar.

49. Tile cleaner—deodorized kerosene (buy at an oil co.).

50. Windshield anti-fog—Glycerin (buy at the drug store).

51. Label cement—egg white is an excellent labeler of cement.

52. Cockroach exterminator—Borax (buy at the grocery store).

53. Ground mole control powder- Black pepper placed liberally in their runs.

54. Battery anti-corrode—Vaseline.

55. Fire extinguisher—plain baking soda.

56. Nail bleach—hydrogen peroxide (buy at the drug store).

57. Type cleaner—rubbing alcohol (buy at the drug store).

58. Wonder car product—removes tar, paint, wax, gum, etc., Benzol.

59. Cures cigarette habit—take before breakfast ½ tsp. each of Rochelle Salts and Cream of Tarter, also chew Ginseng root and swallow the juice.

60. For great beauty—drink a tsp. of Figwort, this will banish every blemish from your skin as it cleanses the blood. Camomile teas will give one a complexion to be proud of.

SEWING:

1. Emergency ripped hem repair—use double faced sticky tape between hem and dress.

2. Bobbins, thread, and other sewing notions can be hung on a bulletin board with straight pins near your machine.

3. Cut buttons, zippers, snaps, hooks, and eyes from all old clothes and place near your sewing machine. Pin all of the buttons that are alike together with a large safety pin. Saves a lot!

4. Cut the cost of making a round tablecloth by using the fringe from an old bedspread.

5. To cover stains on children's clothes, iron transfers of animals, etc., over spots or paint with textile paints. Looks new!

6. To re-line a jacket or coat, use the old lining for the pattern. Spray heavily with starch and press. Pin to the new material for a perfect pattern.

7. for a matched set of spread and drapes, buy two bedspreads and make a set of drapes from one.

8. For an attractive eyeglass case, fold a pot-holder and sew up one side and the end.

9. Worn out tops of little girls slips? Cut off at the waist and insert elastic for half-slip. Also good if she has grown too tall for it.

10. Use iron-on rug binding on men's trousers to prevent "Waist-band curling" of trouser tops. Great for the heavy-set man.

CLOTHING HINTS:

1. Footlets twisted twice in the arch of foot prevents slipping off.

2. Use two rubber bands and three safety pins on sliding bra straps. Pin to each strap and in a "V" to center bra.

3. Use hair spray to stop runs in hose.

4. Clear nail polish will stop runs in hose and also makes good glue.

5. Equal parts of ammonia and turpentine to remove dried paint on clothing.

6. Use nylon net to brush lint off dark clothing.

7. Fold several pieces of tissue, pin through dress with tissues on back to prevent heavy broach from sagging.

8. Felt markers are good to cover shoe scuffs.

9. Grease spots which have set, in washable fabrics, can often be removed by rubbing fresh grease on spot and washing immediately.

Confidential List Of Publications Known To Offer Editorial Write-Ups

This list can mean thousands of dollars in FREE ADVERTISING A YEAR to you if you handle it properly. Items of Products need not necessarily be new in order to obtain these FREE ADVERTISING OR EDITORIAL WRITE-UPS. When contacting these publications enclose a Glossary Photo or drawing of Item and Literature (copy about the item). Tell them you are considering becoming an advertiser in their publications (which you will want to do anyway if the FREE AD pulls well).

Here is the List of Publications and Editorial Columns in which your Free Publicity (Write-Up) can appear:

"POPULAR SCIENCE", 380 Madison Ave., New York, NY 10017 Column: What's New

"POPULAR MECHANICS", 224 West 57th St., New York, NY 10019 Column: New Products

"OUTDOOR LIFE", 380 Madison Ave., New York, NY 10017 Column: What's New

"WORKBENCH", 4251 Pennsylvania Ave., Kansas City, MO 64111 Column: Have You Heard?

"MOTOR TREND", 8490 Sunset Blvd., Los Angeles, CA 90069 Column: New Products and Ideas

"FISHING WORLD", 51 Atlantic Ave., Floral Park, NY 11001 Column: New Products

"PARADE", 750 Third Ave., New York, NY 10017 Column: Parade of Progress

"POWERBOAT", 15917 Strathern St, Van Nuys, CA 91406 Column: What's New Afloat

"SKIN DIVER MAGAZINE", 8490 Sunset Blvd., Los Angeles, CA 90069 Column: New Products

"TOWN AND COUNTRY", 1700 Broadway, New York, NY 10019 Column: R.S.V.P.

"WALLACE'S FARMER", 1501 42nd St., Ste. 501, W. Des Moines, Iowa 50265 Column: Mail Order Editor

"SUNSET", 80 Willow Rd., Menlo Park, CA 94025 Column: Shopping Center

"HIGH FIDELITY", 825 7th Ave., New York, NY 10019 Column: Audio News

"KIWANIS", 3636 Woodview Trace, Indianapolis, IN 46268 Column: Mail Order Editor

"ESQUIRE", 2 Park Ave., New York, NY 10016 Column: Talking Shop

"ELKS", 425 Diversey Pkwy., Chicago, IL 60614 Column: Elks Family Shopper

"HOT ROD", 8490 Sunset Blvd., Los Angeles, CA 90069 Column: What's New

"SPORTS AFIELD", 250 West 55th St., New York, NY 10019 Column: Shopping Afield

"ROTARIAN MAGAZINE", 1600 Ridge Ave., Evanston, IL 60201 Column: Sale By Mail

"SKI", 380 Madison Ave., New York, NY 10017 Column: New Products

"TRUE", 1515 Broadway, New York, NY 10036 Column: True Goes Shopping

When contacting these publications, enclose a description of your item or product in not more than 125 to 140 words.

New Books &
Moneymaking
Opportunities

$12,000 Guaranteed in Just 3 Minutes

by Sam Pitts
Want to receive cash by answering your phone? The author shows you how! Sam says this method of making money with his phone earned him from $400 to $29,000 for each three minute phone call. With this method, he earned $568,554.16 in four months! Many people have tried his program with great success. One man from New York, John Liberto, says "Your money-making secret is ringing my phone off the hook with calls amounting into thousands of dollars." If you would like to have YOUR phone earn you money, order this book.
#0636; $12.95

Thousands of Dollars a Day With Your Camera

by Jeff Peters
How would you like to get paid thousands of dollars for just taking simple pictures? You don't even have to be a skilled photographer to use this revolutionary method of making thousands with your camera. This method is so revolutionary that most photographers have never even heard of this method of making money with your camera. Using this book, you can create for yourself the life you've always wanted: a new home, new car, nice clothes ... for yourself and your family. Follow the simple instructions in this book — just aim your camera, take the picture and the money is yours — it's as simple as that!
#2733; $12.95

How to Use Your Hidden Potential to Get Rich

by David Bendah
Here's the path that self-made millionaires took to make their fortunes, and now you, too, can follow this road to riches. No matter what the level of your skills, intelligence or experience, author David Bendah shows you how to make your personal and financial dreams come true! Don't wait another day to order this book. Find out what hidden potential lies within you!
#0433; $12

How to Achieve Total Success

by Russ von Hoelscher
This exciting book is an owner's manual for your life! It tells you how to create rich, loving, creative, healthy, happy and powerful living. Open your heart to unconditional love, your mind to new awareness, your body to better health and your wallet to ever-increasing wealth! If you're ready for a life-change, then this book is just for you! Order today to begin your new journey with this first step.
#0933; $15

Dropship Directory

by Samuel P. Wood

This is the most up-to-date directory in the United States, with more listing and companies than any other directory. Don't carry costly inventory; deal with companies that will dropship their products directly to YOUR customers, so YOU make more money! If you're in the mail-order business, or plan to be, this directory is a "must have!"

#3725; $15

Taiwan Trade Directory

by Samuel P. Wood

A complete directory of over 10,000 products that you can import from Taiwan. Hundreds of companies listed that will ship products right to your door. Whether it is a custom-made product or a quality standard product-line, you need this directory. Includes pages and pages of: full company addresses, photographs and descriptions of exciting, mail-order industries and gift products. Just up-dated for 1988 and 1989. An excellent source of leads when searching for that "perfect product" to import.

#3726; $15

Hong Kong Import Directory

by Samuel P. Wood

A complete directory of over 100 companies who will ship products to you from Hong Kong. Pages and pages of: company names, addresses, photos and descriptions of exciting mail-order products. The primary source for "hot" items to import for your mail-order business!

#3727; $15

European Import Directory

by Samuel P. Wood

Quality products, made by the craftsmen of old Europe, are available to YOU when you use this directory. Over 100 companies which will ship to you from Europe are listed, with their names, addresses and a complete description of products (including many photos). This collection of import items may hold just the products you've been searching for!

#3728; $15

Cashing In On Government Surplus

by Edward Kelly

NOW is the time to start saving on cars, boats, homes and more! This manual tells you which government sales offer the items YOU want and how to get on their mailing lists. How would you like new cameras, fine wines, liquors and much more, all at fantastic savings? Who wouldn't! Do you want a new car? Exciting, nearly-new cars, such as Porsches and Mercedes, are available at pennies-on-the-dollar! All of these expensive items are waiting for you at the special auctions discussed in this manual. Never been to an auction before? The author helps the novice auction-bidder by giving practical auction-bidding tips. Also, find out which auctions sell homes at fantastic, low prices! Save like never before on repossessed luxury items! Send for this manual today!

#0938; $14.95

$2,000 an Hour

by David Bendah

Would you like to stake a claim to your share of the $25 billion the government holds for you, by just making a few phone calls and looking in some phone books? If you can read English and speak on the phone, you are on your way to making thousands of dollars overnight. People have made up to $2,000 an hour returning money to lost owners! This book shows you how you can make big money helping other people get their money from the government.

#0733; $12.95

Novanetics: The Dawn of a New Era

by David Bendah

Your search is over. You've just found what you've always been looking for. In this two-part series, nationallyrenowned author David Bendah guides you along the path to success and happiness. Book òne tells the secret of *Novanetics* and book two is *Novanetics* in action. A formula for success that is as old as mystical wisdom from the past and as powerful as modern technology is revealed in these books. According to Bendah, there is only one road to absolute success and it is *Novanetics*. Once you are able to master the fundamentals of success, you will be able to master any or all of the three types of success: success with yourself, success with others and success with material things, such as wealth. Do you want to achieve these three types of success? If the answer is *yes,* then you need *Novanetics.*

#9938; $69.95

The Amazing Method Of Reading People

by Tom Foster

Imagine walking into a crowd and being an instant hit just because you know how to "read" women. Read beautiful women instantly with this amazing method. It is easy and effective. If you can tell the difference between a smile and a frown you will be able to use this method. Many government agencies use this sure-fire method of seeing through women.
#0533; $10

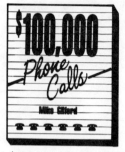

The $100,000 Phone Calls

by Mike Gilford

Could you use $200 an hour for just answering your phone? This kind of cash can be yours for just picking up the receiver and waiting for calls to come in. This is the most revolutionary, money-making system you have ever heard of before. It's a business which allows you to take a 20¢ commission off work you never perform! The people who perform the work are more than willing to give you 20¢ because you will be offering them more jobs than they will have the time to do! This is a service that is really needed. After you receive this book, you too can sit by the TV earning a 20¢ commission while others are out there doing the work for you.
#4933; $10

$4,000 A Day Giving Away Special Books

by Pete Branin

Here is an exciting program that could earn you up to $4,000 a day giving away special books. These special books are a promotional program needed by small businesses. Small businesses have reported increases as much as 500% because of these special books. A man in Florida is making $2,000,000 a year using this special book give-away method. This person has been doing this for five years and is increasing the amount of money he makes every year. This book is based on a $2,000 course, so you know you will get a lot for your money. Cash-in today on "special books."
#1336; $12

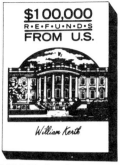

Cutting Into The Billion Dollar Modeling Industry

by Jeff Peters

Are you tired of your boring job? Do you want to make your dreams come true? Imagine making thousands of dollars while meeting an working with beautiful women! Women will beg you to use them in your next "shoot." *Cutting Into the Billion Dollar Modeling Industry* can show you how! In it, author Jeff Peters tells you how to control the most gorgeous and exotic women in the world. He tells you everything you need to know to make money in the modeling business; how the business works; what it takes to be successful; how to begin; how to run your business; how to deal with models and how this new career can change your life. This book can show an individual, regardless of skill or experience, how to start making money in modeling. As soon as you receive your book, you can begin your new career in the glamour business of the 80's. This book is designed to change your life!

#1033; $12.95

How to Get Rich In Multi-Level Marketing

by David Holmes & Joel Andrews

You can get rich without hard work by using this multilevel approach. Your agents get the product from the company, but YOU get the commission from your agents and each agent they enlist! Others do the work while you sit back and collect the commissions.

Thousands of people just like yourself are making more than $100,000 a year without any hard work! Once you have this book, you can begin to create your fortune with any product you choose. Holmes and Andrews have a combined 20-years of experience in sales and marketing. Holmes, a marketing expert and author of two books, has made more than 150 television and radio appearances over the past year. Andrews, who has personally launched six successful business ventures, is so highly regarded in sales and marketing that he has testified on marketing to both houses of Congress. Together, these men teach you how to get rich without hard work!

#1855; $14.95

$100,000 Refunds from the U.S.

by William Kerth

Could you use a share of the hundreds of millions of dollars of government refunds waiting for you? This is a cash windfall which has added $288,000,000 every year to the pot. All you have to do to get this cash windfall is to send off one letter to the address given in this book. One letter and you could be thousands richer! A special office in the federal government housing department is authorizing these refunds. Not only could you be eligible for these government refunds, but if you are not, this book shows you how to get a 30¢ finder's fee for delivering this money to someone who is eligible for a refund. That's hundreds of millions of dollars waiting to go back to the American people! Countless numbers of people are due this money. There are millions in finder's fees you could cash-in on. Get this book today!

#5433; $12.95

The $25 Billion Treasure

by David Bendah

Right now the states are holding billions of dollars of unclaimed money. You could make thousands of dollars by just returning this money to the rightful owners. One man in Texas made over $300,000 from finder's fees on unclaimed money. Studies show that one in ten Americans have unclaimed money coming to them. You could have money owed to you! This book is the greatest manual ever written on getting unclaimed money. It is filled with vital information to help you profit from the government riches of unclaimed money.

#3633; $25

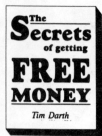

Instant Cash
by Joseph Wright

This five-section, three book series is a MUST for anyone who needs money or needs to get out of debt. Section One will give you information of how to get loans from secretive sources, including foreign and overseas banks. Section Two will show you how to get major credit cards even if you have bad credit. Section Three will show you how to get out of debt · no matter how bad; divorce is this sections specialty. Section Four shows you how to start getting AAA-1 credit rating, which you may use to buy a new business or just an apartment building. Section Five shows you how to get some of the billions of dollars of free money which foundations give away every year. This series knows-all and tells-all about debt and financing. #9933; $29.95

Erase Bad Debt
by Joseph Wright

If you have ever wanted your credit situation turned around, this complete book can do it for you! Erase your debt forever, with this simple and legal, secret method which uses government intervention. The government will get your creditors off your back once and for all, AND you'll never have to pay anyone a cent! Get creditors arrested if they hassle you for money. It makes sure you don't owe anyone a penny and creditors don't bother you. **This isn't bankruptcy!** Also convert your bad debt into AAA-1 credit in a short period of time.
#2940; $15

Getting Free Grants
by Joseph Wright

Do you need some free money this week to pay off some bills or start your own business? Well, look no further because these private foundations I tell you about are loaded with money to give out to individuals just like yourself. I don't care if you're poor and you don't have an extra dollar. These foundations will give you thousands of dollars to help you out or get you a business of your own. One man from Canada, who was laid off from work and who didn't have any insurance for a hospital visit, received thousands of dollars to pay off his hospital bill. If you are poor or don't have enough money, just fill-out the proper forms and you will start receiving thousands of dollars.
#9936; $12

How To Turn Bad Debt Into AAA-1 Credit
by Joseph Wright

You could turn your bad credit into AAA-1 credit in a matter of weeks. You will be amazed at the instant results this guide will get you. By using this complete guide you, too, can turn bad credit into perfect credit. Every time you go to get a loan you will be approved instantly, once they see you have AAA credit. If you never want to be turned down again, order this complete guide.
#9935 $15

How To Raise Millions Of Dollars
by Carl Simon

Would a million dollars be enough to buy the business you have in mind? Are you in need of money to start your own business or some money to start your own company? There are billions of dollars that banks and large corporations would like to invest in your type of business. This complete method of raising millions of dollars will show you how to go about getting big money to start your own venture, which could make you millions every year.
#0634; $15

The Secrets of Getting Free Money
by Tim Darth

By just filling-out a few forms, you could receive thousands of dollars from private institutions all across the country, who must give out free money just to keep their tax status. It is estimated that over 3 billion dollars ($3,000,000,000) is given out every year to people and organizations in need of cash to pay debts or start a new business. Most people don't even know about some of these agencies which are desperately in need of applicants (like yourself) who need money to pay off debts, buy a car or start a new business. If you consider yourself one of these people who need money for practically any purpose, these institutions will get you that money you need. This book tells you who to contact.
#2936; $15

$200,000 in 24 Hours and 130 Other Money Making Reports

by Thomas Brown

Did you ever wonder what companies give you when they offer to make you an instant millionaire overnight? Now for the first time, almost every money-making plan and idea on the market has been compiled into one package for you! This is your chance to make thousands of dollars everyday. You learn how to: *Turn bad credit ratings into AAA-1 credit ratings. *How to make $2,000 an hour with gov't unclaimed money. *Stop paying property taxes forever. *Obtain FREE SUBSCRIPTIONS to over 100 magazines. *FREE FOOD, clothing, furniture and cars! These same systems can produce thousands of dollars with practically no effort on your part. Next month you could have $10,000 in your account. If you need money desperately, this entire collection is for you!
#0333; $10

Capital Raising Digest

by Joseph Wright

So you need mega-bucks? This book will help you find you way through the financing jungle with solid information on raising money both for yourself and for others. This is designed for two types of people: those who want to borrow money for their own use and those who want to establish their own financial brokerage business. You'll learn how to set-up your brokerage business, the ABC's of borrowing, how to read and use financial reports and how to get mega-bucks from lenders outside the country! This is the book you need!
#9934; $15

The Self Publisher's Opportunity Kit

by David Bendah

This exciting book is all you need to make money in mail order. This system **includes** eight books that you can sell by mail! These eight books come with reprint rights, which allow you to reprint and sell as many copies as you wish. One man selling these books is making $14.50 profit on every $15 sale! That's a whopping 3000% profit margin! If this sounds like the right kind of business for you, then this book is the opportunity you've been looking for.
#1633; $30

999 Little Known Businesses That Can Make You a Fortune

by William Carruthers

This book is a collection of 999 businesses that have made their owners rich and they can make you rich, too! The majority of these ideas require little or no capital and can be started in your spare time. *999 Little Known Businesses* gives you such a wide variety of projects to undertake that you are sure to find one, or more, perfect making-making business for you! Start today building your new future with this treasure-trove of information.
#2155; $10

How to Get Rich With Your Micro Computer

by Edwin Simpson

The on-going computer explosion has made the computer affordable to everyone. Now, you can take the computer and put it to work for you... to make you money! This book gives the hopeful computer entre-preneur suggestions on computer-related enterprises and how to profit on them, along with a business primer and advertising sug-gestions. Even the beginner with a computer can put this book to use to make money with an inexpensive computer. Suggested businesses and thorough explanations ensure that, with a computer and this book, you can't lose.
#1730; $12

Making $500,000 A Year In Mail Order

by David Bendah
If you've ever dreamed of having your mailbox crammed with thousands of envelopes, each containing a check in your name, or if your dream is working any hours you want, whenever you want, then this book is for you! Bendah's mail order book will help you get the pleasures that life has to offer. Your dreams can become a reality because mail-order is one of the most lucrative businesses you can have. This book is full of helpful, easy-to-understand information on creating success in this field. Bendah, considered one of the nation's leading writers, teaches laymen how best to use his unique techniques and explains every aspect of book formation and marketing. He discloses his secret formula which has ensured the success of many mail order businesses. This book can be your key to mailorder success.
#1233; $15

How to Get Rich In Mail Order

by Melvin Powers
You can learn what to do and what not to do in starting your own mail order business from the voice of experience: Melvin Powers. He is a book publisher and mail order entrepreneur who has worked this profitable business for over 25 years. In this book, he shares what he has learned and tell you how you can be successful in this field. Powers shows you how to be creative and, therefore, profitable. This book shows you strategies for success, along with practical advice on marketing, advertising and finding a product and service to sell. It is full of samples and examples, so the information is easy to learn. As a bonus, Powers tells you how to sell on television. The variety of subjects covered makes this a valuable reference source for the person interested in the mail order business.
#2655; $20

$15,000 for "Free Shopping"

by Brad Nolin
Imagine taking home $15,000 each time you go shopping free. That's right, $15,000 for simple shopping that won't cost you a red cent! One man who lives in California became a millionaire overnight using the exact system explained in this book. He now takes home $3,000,000 a year. Could you use $15,000 for doing some simple shopping? Brad Nolin reveals his incredible method for making this dream a reality. This is a whole new life of wealth and happiness for you!
#4833; $10

Make a Fortune and Travel Absolutely Free

by Ben & Nancy Dominitz
Have you hears about the fat commission checks and free travel benefits in the travel industry? This book reveals how you can get both without using a dime of your own money. This book shows you how to: * Start your travel business out of your home in your spare time * Add a minimum of 50% to your present income * Travel free, a guest of air and cruise lines and tour companies * Receive a discount on all airline tickets and hotel bills * Make a fortune with group travel and much, much more. Use this book to start a new, profitable business or just to save money on all your travels!
#1955; $20

Cashing In On Govt Money
by Bill Kerth
Could you use at least $30,000 that is owed to you by Uncle Sam and is available to you, just for the asking? Imagine receiving check after check just for filling-out the proper forms! There are many government programs for 1988 and 1989, that you have probably never even heard of, which could make you rich. You could buy a new home for just $1.00. Uncle Sam foots the rest of the bill! How about getting the government to buy you a McDonald's franchise? What could YOU get?
#5033; $12.95

Getting the Government to Pay for Your Real Estate
by Jack E. Gates
Real Estate *by Jack E. Gates* The U.S. Government gives away grants and guarantees loans for real estate ventures. Just imagine you could now have the dream home you've always wanted, even if you could NOT afford it! If it's investment real estate that you're after, the government can help you with this, too.   Right now, get your share of government real estate money!
#3863; $13.95

How To Get Free Grants From The U.S. Government
by Tim Darth
Could you use a $35,500 free-money grant right from the government, which you do not have to pay back? By just filling out a few forms they provide you with, you could be on your way to receiving this grant. The government will even give you a $5,000 grant just to fix up your home. Uncle Sam has billions of dollars that he gives away every year to people who need money. You could be receiving thousands of dollars right from the government to do practically anything. You can even get a fifty thousand dollar grant to help you write your first hit song! You can also get thousands of free grants for certain businesses. They will pay part of your rent just to live in an apartment. Just fill out the forms, and you're on your way.
#4861; $15

Become a Real Estate Millionaire
by Phillip Wellington
Here is the big picture of what's possible for YOU in the world of real estate. In this book, the author gets you started with the insider terms that will open doors for you. You get special knowledge of the inner workings of the property-game, including: tax advantages, capitalization and cash-flow. You learn how to get rich using other people's money. Buy valuable, commercial property for "no down." How do you find the best investment properties, such as rental units? This book gives YOU all the insiders' tips on finding, financing, renovating and maintaining rentals... and keeping them rented! Want to grow even larger? Use leap-frogging to increase your financial clout. Make your investments grow right before your eyes with the knowledge gained from this book!
#3862; $15

Buying Real Estate At Government Public Auctions
by Jack E. Gates
The government auctions-off billions of dollars worth of goods every year at give-away prices. One auction can put thousands of dollars in your pocket. New houses, land, apartments, all go for pennies on the dollar. My insider guide shows you how you can buy these properties at rock-bottom prices and then turn around and sell them for huge profits! Each day you could make up to a thousand dollars or more. If you would like to get rich, the government will give you the property, so why wait?
#2937; $15

Work At Home Riches

by John Collins

Tired of working for someone else? Then it's time to create your own business at home and make MONEY! This sourcebook is a complete guide for home-based work, giving you insider secrets such as which businesses to get into and suggestions on how to set-up your business. Valuable information includes: * How to market your product or service * Over 300 work-at-home sources * Insurance for the home business * Tax and zoning codes * How to run a successful mail-order business * Over 30 FREE publicity sources * Over 60 drop-shippers, plus prices and product description AND MUCH, MUCH MORE! If you plan a home business, then this book is a "must have!"
#0888; $15

Insider Home Business Riches

by John Collins

Imagine getting paid for calling people up and asking them a few questions. Thanks to the "Insider Home Business Riches," I have some firms that will pay you to call on people and ask them a few simple questions. I have even found some firms that will pay you a monthly check just to ask for donations of household items that are discarded from the home. There are people who are making thousands of dollars right out of their homes and getting a big monthly check from a large corporation. Would you like to sit at home and make good money?

#0889; $15

Stay Home and Make Money

by Russ von Hoelscher

Full-time or spare-time, you can start making big profits in the safety and comfort of your own home. This exciting book presents you with scores of new, proven, profitable ways to have your cake and eat it too. This is really four books in one: 1) How to get started right and avoid the pitfalls 2) Home business opportunities that are hot right now; moneymaking plans 3) Writing/publishing services that people want and will pay you handsomely for (writing experience unnecessary) 4) Special, big profit opportunities in direct marketing and mail order AND MUCH, MUCH MORE!
#2656; $15

Take Your Junk Mail to the Bank

by Larry Miller

Don't laugh at this idea, you CAN take your junk mail and "turn it into cash." The junk mail you receive in your home could be worth thousands of dollars! This manual tells you how you could be making up to $1,500 or more, simply by filling out a form and putting it into the mail. If you get 10 pieces of junk mail a week, you could get back $350 a week. So, that means that 20 to 100 pieces might bring $700 to $3,500 next week! Send for this manual today to learn how to "turn your junk mail into cash."
#0637; $12

Unique Packages

by David Bendah

Can you imagine making at least $50,000 this week? What about $250,000 this month? With this amazing system, you CAN! All you do is distribute "unique packages" that you are supplied absolutely free! This book explains how the system works. This idea is new, fresh and badly needed in this country. It will make the American dream become a reality for you. Order this book today and start enjoying the luxuries the "Unique Packages" system can get for you.
#1335; $12

Building Your Million Dollar Empire

by Mike Gilford

Everyone knows that the key to making large amounts of money lies in real estate. You can practically buy real estate for nothing down and, in some cases, you can get money back for buying some real estate! This book shows you how to get into real estate without cash. Real estate is a solid investment... an investment that will increase in value for years to come. This is an investment that can make you a millionaire! You must own a piece of America if you truly want to build your million dollar empire. Start today by ordering this amazing book. #5133; $10

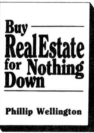

Buy Real Estate With Nothing Down

by Phillip Wellington

Here's how you can have a real estate empire using no money of your own! Get your feet wet in the real estate market, without any cash. This book tells it all. You'll find out how, with little or no money down, you can buy real estate without using any of your own money! Here, you'll get insider information on all the traditional ways to finance PLUS all the exciting, new ways to raise money. Learn how to negotiate a deal with the property seller, use equity sharing and leverage. Also, find out how to actually get the seller to HELP YOU with the financing! Phillip Wellington's system tells you how. Order today to get started buying real estate with nothing down. #3858; $15

Getting $1 Homes From the U.S. Government

by Phillip Wellington

As incredible as it sounds, it IS possible to buy your own property for only one dollar! The Department of Housing and Urban Development (HUD) repossesses close to five thousand home per month! A percentage of these homes fall into a category called the "Urban Homestead Program." One of the only requirements for home-buyers considering this approach is that you must live at the property in question for five years. If there is any renovation to be done, you must do them within three years. Any way you look at it, this is the opportunity of a life-time! Get your $1 home before they are all gone.

#2945; $10

Cashing In On Foreclosures

by Jack E. Gates

Would you like to start bringing in thousands of dollars every month just by finding foreclosures in your city? I have seen people buy one house and then turn around and sell it for $8,000 to $25,000 in profit in less than three month's time. Once you see the insider secrets for making million s in the real estate business, you'll know why there is no better way to get rich faster than with foreclosed property. Every month there are over 5,000 houses, which go into foreclosure, that you can pick-up for bargain basement prices. Whether you would like to buy your first house or have a positive cash flow of thousands of dollars a month, you'll have the insider sources of where to find all these great houses at great prices. #3891; $15

The Ultimate Method of Making Instant Cash

by Bob Kelly
Here is a program in which you can make as much as $10,000 for every special box you have. These 12" high moneymakers are earning thousands of people money for just having one of these special boxes. These colorful boxes really collect money for you, while you're watching TV at home! The number of people who can make money with these boxes is limited, because the boxes are set-up in territories. One box and an instruction book is included with this program. Everything you need to get into business immediately is included with the box package. You can literally make money within 15 minutes of getting this package! There is a $3 UPS charge with this program and you must include a street address for UPS shipment (NOT a Post Office Box number).
#6633; $12

You Can Make Millions In the Import/Export Market

by Samuel P. Wood
Join the world market with these two books! In the first book, you receive easy-to-follow information on setting up your business, finding a name, getting the right product to sell and finding and contacting suppliers. You get insider information on mail-order sales and how and when to advertise. Learn the exciting world of drop-ship selling and how to make more sales with less time and effort. The second book includes two sections: "The Government and You" and "Finding Capital." You'll learn about transportation, orders and payments and getting the maximum profit for your import. Extensive lists of capital sources, foreign embassies, U.S. Custom offices and exporters/manufacturers complete this extensive book.
#3729; (Two books) $29.95

Winning at the Horse Races

by Paul Lawrence
Can you imagine knowing exactly which horse will finish first, before the race starts? This system could put millions of dollars in your pocket every year! It is a 27-part, scientific system that is guaranteed to give you results. If you have a calculator and five minutes, you're in business. You could be picking winning horses with this method. Become the racetrack guru with this amazing method!
#1933; $19.95

How to Find Anyone, Anywhere

by Ted Green
This invaluable book gives you the information you need to help you find anyone you're looking for anywhere, for any purpose: children lost through adoption, birthparents, long-lost relatives, ex-spouses, childhood friends, or just someone who owes you money! The author gives you insight into using advanced techniques, many of the same techniques used by the pros, whose careers are dependent upon finding people! Some of the information includes computer and national listings, courthouse listings, occupational listings and much, much more! If you've ever wanted to find someone, then THIS is the book you need to find anyone, anywhere!
#1559; $15

Seminar Riches

by Phil Jones
Can you talk to people and tell them a story? If you can, I'm going to show you how, by just opening your mouth, you can be on the road to riches quicker than you can imagine. Other people are making thousands everyday just giving seminars in their own cities. I know one guy by the name of Robert in San Diego who puts on a seminar for seven days. He has 200 people attending every other week, and he brings in $900,000 the week he does two seminars. Would you like to have that kind of money for just opening your mouth?
#2934; $19.95

How To Set Up Your Own Million-Dollar Business

by Pat Telino
Could you run your own business and make hundreds of thousands of dollars every year? Millions of dollars are being made every year by people who have just started their own business. People are getting rich by setting up ordinary businesses that are growing to enormous levels. One man started a mail order business that now does over 3 million dollars a year in sales. Another man started a telemarketing business right from scratch, and it is doing over 2 million dollars a year. With this million dollar business you could be on your way to a million dollar year.
#2935; $14.95

Grey Market Riches

by Dan Webster
Beautiful Porsches, as well as Mercedes, could be parked in front of your house and could be earning you as much as $20,000 each! Did you ever dream that driving luxury cars could make you so much money? This book will show you how to buy almost any luxury car overseas at a fraction of what it costs in this country. Buy cars overseas without leaving your home. All you have to do is make a simple call to Europe and $20,000 is yours. It's as easy as that!
#1733; $19.95

Product Millions

by Samuel P. Wood
Isn't it time you joined the world market and started on your way to making millions? This series of three books and three directories tells you all you need to know to set-up a thriving import/export business, including: choosing a company name, finding the right product to sell, creating mail-order sales, drop-ship selling and how to make more sales with less time and effort. The author also tells you about how to approach the government so that Uncle Sam works FOR you, not against you; how to handle transportation, orders, payments and how to get maximum profit from your import. If finding capital is a problem, then the section on financing will get you going. This book also covers working with foreign embassies, chambers of commerce, US Customs offices and exporters/manufacturers. The final book on marketing gives you all the insider tips on how to successfully advertise and move your selected product. You even find out how to get free advertising and promotion to help you on your way to millions!
#155; $295

Couponing Association

This complete package contains a sales kit, demonstration kit, "Special Books" manual (a complete guide to running a successful coupon business) and sample forms: three contracts and one insertion order. Included is the consultation phone number for assistance, offered to couponing association members only. Why go-it-alone when so much professional help is available?
#166; $49

Money Finder's Association

Members of this association are offered three booklets to assist them:
 1) States Reports—which gives detailed information on the rules and regulations (from every state) concerning unclaimed money
 2) Legal Contracts—including several power-of-attorney, twoparty agreement contracts, which were drawn-up by lawyers
 3) Finding Unclaimed Porperty—which gives information on how to locate people, how to approach them in correspondence and in person and how to set-up your own unclaimed property business
 BONUS: As a member, you also get the Money Finder's Association Newsletter and the phone number for a consultant's line, available to members only.
#133; $99

Poor Man's Way To Riches, Volume 1
by David Buckley

The first volume of this valuable series will help you clear off old debts and start on your new financial future.

It will tell you how to : • Make a Million Dollars in Real Estate • Take Over Going Businesses With Zero Cash • Earn $5,000 Monthly by Mail • One-Man Businesses That Can Make You Rich • How to Avoid Taxes Legally, and more!
#3033; $10

Volume 2

Volume 2 tells you how to: Earn $30,000 Monthly From Oil Income • Get a Cash Loan From Your State • Obtain Foundation Grants and Loans • Build a $20,000 Coin Collection From Pennies • Enter a Lottery You Can't Lose • Get 24% on Your Savings • Seven Offshore Big Money Lenders • Cash in on Arab Money • Free Patents From NASA
#3133; $10

Volume 3

Volume 3 tells you how to: Turn 1,000 Into $250,000 • $100,000 in 90 Days With Discount Books • Become a New Car Broker • $500,000 Yearly From Cordwood Sales • Sell $2,000 Memberships in Survival Retreats • Make $50,000 a Year With a Newsletter Digest • Roll in Profits With Electric Vehicles • Sell Solar Energy Systems • Make $300,000 Yearly With Strategic Metals.
#3233; $10

Volume 4

Volume 4 tells you how to: Make $20,000 a Month With Debt Consolidation • $1,200 a Week With ID Cards • A Business Making $60,000 a Day • Sell Platinum from Auto Catalytic Converters • Grow Big Bucks From Jojoba Farming • Make $1,950 Daily From Photography • Invest in Pennies and Confederate Money • Make Huge Commissions as a Patent Broker • $150,000 Yearly as a manufacturers Representative • $25,000 Part-time from Senior Service • How to Make $4,600 in Five Days.
#3333; $10

Making Millions From Free Products
by George F. Strong

You could find free products that could make you millions every year. Products that you thought had no value could be sold for thousands. Besides getting free products you are taught how to get free advertising. The company that sold the "Pet Rock" sold one million rocks without one cent of advertising money. This is one of the best books you will ever come across.
#3730; $15

$1,000,000 Cashvision
by Jeff Peters

Imagine watching TV while you are making money! Watching your favorite shows could pay off for you with this book, which shows you how to make money with your favorite TV shows. A man from California made a whooping $9,000,000 in one year from TV shows! Another man, from Arizona, made over $4,000,000 with the same program that is outlined in this book. Everyone can now cash-in on their TV set. Why watch TV for nothing when you can use "cashvision" to make you rich?
#2744; $12.95

Direct Response Millions

by David Bendah

Complete, six volume kit for creating your own, directmail company. Over ten years of trial and error by the author has gone into this system. He discovered the insider secrets to making over $2,000,000 per year in direct mail and now YOU can profit from that experience. David Bendah is a nationally renowned expert who can show you how to make a fortune by mail. His six-volume set covers: display and classified ads, how to sell by direct mail, getting free advertising, choosing your product, TV & radio advertising, how to get help from the government and much more! Let Bendah's expertise help you get started on your road to riches today! #177; Six Vol. Set $295

Wholesale Book Dealership

by David Bendah

How would you like to make over $20,000 a week selling books by mail, like nationally-renowned Publisher David Bendah does? He believes there is no better way to get rich faster than by selling books by mail—exciting, money-making books that he supplies to YOU! Here's your chance to become one of his exclusive dealers, with discounts up to 70% off all of the books in this catalog! He offers you this New Horizon Catalog and you don't have to handle any inventory. Bendah will drop-ship the books to your customers. With this dealership, you get: * The right to sell over 100 quality paperback and hard-bound books, many of them sold in bookstores * Discounts of up to 70% off all the books in this catalog * FREE book: *"Making $500,000 a Year In Mail Order,"* hardbound, 200 pages, 6" X 9" * FREE, the kit you've been waiting for: *Self-Publisher's Opportunity Kit,* approx. 200 pages, 8 1/2" X 11" * FREE four exciting audio cassette tapes to re-enforce your information and learning * FREE, best-selling, camera-ready ads, from the Opportunity Showcase, which YOU can print-up and reproduce to increase your sales! * News of the latest book releases; books I have tested to be proven winners! * Drop-shipping of all my books to your customers, without you doing ANY work! Dealerships are limited, so order yours today, while they're still available.
#111; (Entire Book Dealership package, plus two books & four tapes) $99

Real Estate Millions

by Phillip Wellington

How would you like to have a monthly income of over $20,000? That's right, you could have a monthly income TODAY in excess of $20,000 from your real estate holdings! With this six-book system, you learn how to take-over property that's worth a fortune, and yet put only a few dollars down. It will astound you once you see how easy it is to take over these real estate properties using practically no money of your own! In this system, you gain information to get you started to create your own real estate empire, then continue on to use creative financing, let the government pay your way and learn to buy wholesale with bankruptcies and auctions. These books also tell you how to find and buy money-saving foreclosures and how to build great wealth with commercial real estate. Order this entire series of guarded insider secrets and government programs, today!
#188; Six Vol. Set $199

Let The U.S. Government Make Your Fortune In Real Estate

by Phillip Wellington

How would you like to build a real estate empire, with the help of the government backing-you-up 100%? Our government practically gives away millions upon millions of dollars worth of money for real estate every year. These government programs can give you riches beyond your belief. I'm talking about $1.00 homes right from the government, and $5,000 in free money to fix it up. Just one of these agencies can give you the money to build the home of your dreams or any brand-new house you would like to live in. One of the biggest promoters of real estate is the U.S. government, and they can make you rich by giving you the money to buy any real estate you like.
#3859; $15

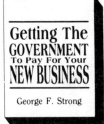

Getting the Government to Pay for Your New Business

by George F. Strong

How about some money to start your own business or buy a franchise like Burger King© or Wendy's©? The government will get you that first business or franchise, which can start making you millions of dollars. Every day of the year the government gives out millions of dollars to people who want to start their own business or buy a franchise which they would like to own. I know of one many from Houston, Texas, who received all the money he needed from Uncle Sam to buy two Mc Donald© franchises. He did it through a little-known, new government program. Would you like Uncle Sam to buy you a McDonald's©? Then, you need this book!
#4055; $14.95

Getting Rich With Foreclosures

by Phillip Wellington

Learn how to take advantage of bankruptcy sales, Veterans Administration repossessed property sales and much more! This dynamic book lists all of the many government auctions and summarizes each for YOU. How much do you know about U.S. Customs Service auctions, local police auctions, U.S. Post Office auctions, trustee sales, sheriff's sales and tax sales? The author has bought over 14 houses and numerous cars at such auctions. This books shows how YOU can save at these auctions. Order today to start saving!
#3861; $15

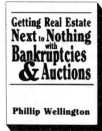

Getting Real Estate Next to Nothing with Bankruptcies and Auctions

by Phillip Wellington

Would you like to start picking up some of the best bargains in the country? How about a home for $1.00 or an apartment complex at giveaway prices? You could start bringing in thousands everyday just by buying at give-away prices and selling for huge profits. One guy I know, Gary Silver, bought a car at one of these auctions for $320. If you would like to start picking up some great bargains, there is no better place than at bankruptcy auctions which occur everyday in your city.
#3860; $15

Making Money From Display and Classified Ads

by George F. Strong
Learn the insider secrets of display and classified advertising for your direct mail business in this comprehensive book. Would you like to know how to word you ad so that the reader has no choice but to buy your product? Which part of the newspaper will get you 10 times the ad cost in results? This book tells you these facts and much more! Some of the information includes: * What to place in the headline of your ad to triple ad sales * What to place in the coupon to make sure twice as many people send you money right away * What words in a classified ad will get you thousands of dollars for practically nothing * How to cut your ad cost by as much as 50% in many publications, MORE! #4051; $15

Making TV and Radio Advertising Pay Off

by George F. Strong
Would you like to know how to get national coverage of your product for only $15 a minute? What products sell like crazy on cable TV? What airing times will increase your sales 13 times? These answers and much more are in George F. Strong's book on TV and radio advertising. Also covered is: * How to make millions a month selling by TV * A method of getting free air time for your product * What type of program is a hot money-maker * Six subliminal ways to get people to order your product * Which stations will save you thousands AND MUCH, MUCH MORE! Order today to make radio and TV pay off for you! #4052; $15

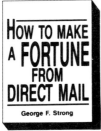

How to Make a Fortune from Direct Mail

by George F. Strong
If you've always wanted to start your own business and get paid everyday, then you'll never have a better chance than by starting your own mail-order business. This book gives you a direct mail overview and specific information on planning your campaign and creating a direct mail package. Learn about the importance of mailing lists in this "age of information," including generating your own lists and making big bucks from them! This tells you about printing, what to look for and how to avoid trouble. After your direct mail piece is printed, how do you test its effectiveness? Chapter six tells you several effective testing methods and chapter seven gives you insider's secrets on fulfilling customers orders to make you money. #4050; $15

How To Advertise Your Business And Sell Products

by Pat Telino
Did you know that with a unique advertising publicity technique you could promote just one product to millions of potential buyers without risking one cent? By using this advertising technique you could make a million dollars in no time at all without putting up one cent. This specific, insider technique has been used by many starting millionaires who are now raking-in millions of dollars every year. Once you see how you can get any product you might have in the hands of millions of buyers without putting up a penny, you'll never worry about having enough buyers again.

#2938; $14.95

Ordering Information

United States Orders

Postage is $1.50 (min.) and 5% of order for an order over $30.00 Special Fourth Class delivery

For UPS a charge of $5.00 must accompany each order.

Please call customer Service if other shipping arrangements are requested.

Enclose check, money order, or credit card information with each order form. We can not accept COD's or open accounts.

Shipments are usually dispatched within three working days of receipt of order.

If a book you ordered is not in stock we will issue you a credit

California residents must include 6% sales tax. (Other states as necessary.)

All Orders Outside USA

1. Postage and handling charge of $4.00 or 5% of total (whichever is greater) must accompany each order.
2. Shipments are by parcel post book rates, surface mail, unless other shipping arrangements are made. Allow 8-10 weeks for delivery.
3. We also accept bank checks drawn on USA banks in USA dollars and Visa and MasterCard.

Our Guarantee

If for any reason you are not completely satisfied with your purchase, just return the merchandise in 60 days, in salable condition, for a prompt credit or refund...no questions asked.

Please send me the following books:

Quantity	Title	Catalog#	Price

n Publishing Company
50 Mission Gorge Road, Suite 222, San Diego, CA 92120

9) 285-9888

☐ Check Enclosed   ☐ MoneyOrder
☐ Visa   ☐ MasterCard

ct. # _____

Subtotal	
Postage	
State tax (if applicable)	
Total	

Signature _____ Exp. Date _____

Name _____ Phone# ( ) _____

Address _____

City/State/Zip _____

NOTES

NOTES

NOTES

NOTES